ESSENTIALS

KELLY D. KING

MINISTRY TO WOMEN

THE ESSENTIAL GUIDE FOR LEADING
WOMEN IN THE LOCAL CHURCH

LifeWay Press® Nashville, Tennessee

EDITORIAL TEAM
ADULT MINISTRY
PUBLISHING

Faith Whatley
Director, Adult Ministry

Michelle Hicks
*Manager, Adult Ministry
Short Term Bible Studies*

Sarah Doss
Content Editor

Lindsey Bush
Production Editor

Heather Wetherington
Art Director

Bekah Wertz
Cover Design

Published by LifeWay Press®
© 2018 LifeWay Christian Resources
Reprinted November 2018

ISBN: 978-1-5359-0289-2 • Item: 005803545

Dewey decimal classification: 259

Subject headings: CHURCH WORK WITH WOMEN / WOMEN / MINISTRY

Unless indicated otherwise, all Scripture taken from the Christian Standard Bible®, Copyright © 2017 by Holman Bible Publishers. Used by permission. Christian Standard Bible® and CSB® are federally registered trademarks of Holman Bible Publishers. Scripture quotations from THE MESSAGE. Copyright © by Eugene H. Peterson 1993, 1994, 1995, 1996, 2000, 2001, 2002. Used by permission of NavPress. All rights reserved. Represented by Tyndale House Publishers, Inc.

Permission is granted to reproduce pages 122-135 for use within your ministry.

To order additional copies of this resource, write to LifeWay Church Resources Customer Service; One LifeWay Plaza; Nashville, TN 37234; order online at www.lifeway.com; fax 615.251.5933; phone toll free 800.458.2772; email orderentry@lifeway.com; or visit the LifeWay Christian Store serving you.

Printed in the United States of America

Adult Ministry Publishing • LifeWay Church Resources • One LifeWay Plaza • Nashville, TN 37234

CONTENTS

ABOUT THE AUTHOR

Kelly D. King is the Women's Ministry Specialist for LifeWay Christian Resources where she coordinates training and equipping events for women in leadership. She holds a Master of Theology degree from Gateway Seminary and was an adjunct professor at Oklahoma Baptist University while serving as the Women's Specialist for the Baptist General Convention of Oklahoma for eleven years. She served as the Women's Ministry Director at Council Road Baptist in Bethany, Oklahoma, and currently leads the women's ministry as a volunteer at Green Hill Church in Mount Juliet, Tennessee.

She and her husband, Vic, have been married thirty years and have served together in ministry, both teaching students and young adults. They have two young adult children, Conner and Courtney, and a son-in-love, Gaige. They enjoy kayaking, having people in their home, and cheering for the Oklahoma Sooners. Kelly is a fan of Tex-Mex and coconut milk mocha macchiatos, but not at the same time.

INTRODUCTION

I have a pretty good idea you picked up this book looking for answers. And I have a pretty good idea you desire to be equipped in your calling to minister to women. Maybe it's been a gentle nudge from the Lord that won't go away. Maybe you were recruited to lead women in your church. Maybe you felt a little coerced and someone handed you this book in hopes it would be of help. Maybe you've even said the phrase I've heard many times—"I'm not even sure I like women!" Whatever the case, I'm hoping you see yourself as a servant leader, called by the Lord. I'm hoping you're excited about this adventure called ministry to women.

Perhaps you aren't a new leader. Maybe you've ministered to women for years, and you're thinking, *Do I need another book on ministry to women?* If that's a question you're asking, let me assure you the answer is *yes*. Women's ministry, or ministry to women, is constantly evolving in the local church. The *why* of ministering to women hasn't changed. The biblical mandate is found in Titus 2—the mother passage of all women's ministry:

> **In the same way, older women are to be reverent in behavior, not slanderers, not slaves to excessive drinking. They are to teach what is good, so that they may encourage the young women to love their husbands and to love their children, to be self-controlled, pure, workers at home, kind, and in submission to their husbands, so that God's word will not be slandered.**
>
> TITUS 2:3-5

Yes, women are instructed to teach younger women and to live worthy of their calling. But the calling to ministry is found in the basic instructions of the Greatest Commandment and the Great Commission. Every Christ follower is called to love the Lord God with all her heart, soul, and mind and love others as herself—the Greatest Commandment. Every Christ follower is called to make disciples who make disciples—the Great Commission. Your calling isn't narrow or easy. Your calling is challenging, global, and full of eternal consequences.

Though our calling is the same as it was for the early church, our methods in the twenty-first century are completely different. In the past ten years, there have been seismic shifts in our Western culture and even in ministry. Part of this may be attributed to the rise of the largest generation to emerge on the scene yet—the

Millennial generation—those born somewhere between 1980 and 2000. Part of the shift is due to the exponential changes in communication—social media, video, and the various ways we interact. We have transitioned to a digital age. Women want rapid and practical applications to learn from God's Word.

Because we live in a digital age, people are struggling more and more with work and life balance. Ministry needs to have flexibility—options and availability for today's woman. In other words, a Bible study offered once a week during the day just isn't going to cut it in our current climate. We, as a society, value collaboration more than ever, which means working in teams carries significant implications. Teams will work collaboratively because one individual doesn't have all the information. We will all learn from each other.

We have shifted from a modern culture to a post-modern culture. No longer does our culture have an inherently biblical worldview or a view of God and the church. In fact, many people seem to go through life without an understanding of who God is or a desire for any type of religion. We call these the "nones"—the number of Americans who do not identify with any religion. According to Pew Research, "one-fifth of the U.S. public—and a third of adults under 30—are religiously unaffiliated today, the highest percentages ever recorded in Pew Research Center polling."[1] We've seen another shift in the rise of women in higher education. In 2006, *The New York Times* reported only 42 percent of college students were male, as compared to 58 percent women. Women are now outpacing men in graduation rates and grade performance.[2] Leadership, in general, has changed. No longer do you see positional leadership, but ministry leaders who manage through influence. Ministry leaders in today's culture guide as coaches, not directors or bosses.

Finally, part of the shift may be attributed to the rise of interest among women as leaders—both in the church and in the marketplace. In a world where female leaders were once few and far between, they are now celebrated and given expanding opportunities to make a difference in the marketplace and in our ministries. The daily news often focuses on issues relating to women—both positive and negative. Whether the issues focus on women's marches, sexual harassment in the workplace, inequality of pay, or myriad issues relating to women, there are lots of opinions that impact the need and emphasis for churches to provide biblical answers and ministry for women.

Let's be clear up front, this book is not a comprehensive resource—it's not meant to be. It's not an encyclopedia or theological dissertation on the roles of women in the church. It's the "essentials"—the things we deem most necessary to include when developing a ministry to women in the local church. The word *essential* is defined as, "basic, indispensable, necessary."[3] In this small book you will find several lists and bullet points to help you think through next steps. They are meant to be practical with simple how-tos and best practices you can easily apply. Each local congregation is different, and there is no one-size-fits-all handbook that will work for every church. So whether you are a church of one hundred or one thousand, a church serving in a rural area or an urban area, a church that is traditional or contemporary (or both), consider this to be a resource that focuses on the broad strokes and not the details, a tool you must adapt to your unique situation. Customize the ideas you read in the following pages to fit your context. Highlight the main things you want to do, and strike through things that don't line up with the direction you are headed. I'm excited you have allowed me the opportunity to speak into your calling. I believe it's a great time to be a woman and a leader in the local church. Whether you are leading a Bible study, planning an event, directing a non-profit, or planning strategic mission initiatives, women are vital to the success of local church ministry.

Women—we need you. The church needs you—both the global church and the local church. And while this isn't the end-all book for your leadership journey, my desire is that it will provide some basic answers to your questions and give you direction as you follow the Lord's calling to minister to women. I'm cheering you on as you pursue God's mission.

CHAPTER 1

START WITH WHY:

PRAYER AND PURPOSE

———

In 2009, Simon Sinek released his book, *Start with Why: How Great Leaders Inspire Everyone to Take Action*. His TEDx Talk®, based on the book, has more than 39 million views, the third most popular TED Talk ever watched to date. Sinek's simple premise: every inspired leader begins with the question of *why* and not *how* or *what*.[1] Your ministry to women must begin with that same question. It's not just a matter of how to start a ministry to women in your local church but a matter of why God gives us a biblical mandate to reach women, disciple them, and encourage them to start the cycle again. When you define the why, your ministry begins with purpose. But it also must begin with prayer.

If I were to ask you who the greatest leader in the Bible is, I hope you would use the standard Jesus answer. He knew His mission. He knew His purpose, and He carried it out. But let's consider other great leaders in the Bible. Moses led the Israelites out of Egypt—no easy task. Peter, along with the other apostles and the indwelling of the Holy Spirit, led the early church even in the midst of great persecution. There is no question that their why was Jesus' instruction to take the gospel to the ends of the earth. I could go on and on with a list of great leaders, but there is one cupbearer to the king who always captures my attention in regard to his focus on purpose and prayer. His name was Nehemiah.

The first chapter of the Book of Nehemiah is the Simon Sinek chapter of Scripture, although I'm not convinced Sinek includes the foundation of prayer in his thesis. Instead, in Nehemiah, we find a dedicated servant who had a relentless burden to rebuild the wall of Jerusalem that had been destroyed by the Babylonians.

Nehemiah's burden and holy discontent wasn't just about a physical wall that would protect Israel from her enemies. It was a spiritual concern for a nation who continued to adopt the religious practices and culture of surrounding ungodly nations. Instead of God's people shaping culture, the culture was shaping them. Sound familiar?

As you consider the spiritual needs of women in your church, ask yourself these questions:

- **DO I HAVE A BURDEN FOR THE WOMEN IN MY CHURCH?** Do I go to church and see women who have a need to connect with God's Word and with each other? Am I aware of the number of women who sit alone in a pew every Sunday morning desiring to connect with others in their pursuit to learn more about the Lord? Do I have a burden for women who walk through the doors of my church who are hurting and broken? Do I seek to develop relationships with women of all ages and stages of life?

- **DO I CARE ABOUT LOST WOMEN IN MY COMMUNITY?** Do I consider the lostness in my community and pray for those who need a relationship with Christ? Am I actively having conversations with women who are far from God? Do I see culture shaping the lives of women in my community or does God's eternal and infallible Scripture shape them and the way they live?

- **ARE MY CONCERNS BASED ON BUILDING SOMETHING THAT WILL BRING RECOGNITION TO ME OR GLORY TO GOD?** Do I seek a position within the church, or am I more concerned with serving the Lord? Am I willing to serve without pay or a title? Eric Geiger, former senior vice president of LifeWay Christian Resources, once said, "The idolatry of ministry is when I'm more concerned about what God is doing through me than what God has already done for me."[2]

- **DOES MY CONCERN FOR WOMEN IN MY CHURCH KEEP ME UP AT NIGHT?** Do I care more about the transformation of women through the gospel than I care about adding a program to the church calendar?

If these questions resonate with you, be encouraged. More than likely, God has placed a holy discontent in your heart to start a ministry to women. So where do you start? Here are some simple steps to help you develop a why for your ministry.

BEGIN WITH PRAYER.

Just as Nehemiah began with prayer, take time to seek the Lord for direction. Nehemiah understood God's character (Neh. 1:4-7), was acquainted with God's promises (vv. 8-9), and had seen God's practices (vv. 10-11). Include a small group of women who share your burden. Pray together. Pray for wisdom. Don't overcomplicate it—just pray and seek the Lord.

MEET WITH THOSE IN AUTHORITY.

As Nehemiah met with King Artaxerxes in Nehemiah 2, consider those with whom you need to meet. Most importantly, connect with your senior pastor or the staff person whose responsibility includes discipleship. Share your burden and seek their input and support. Consider how your vision lines up with the overall mission of your church and explain how your women's ministry will only enhance what is currently happening.

ASSESS THE NEEDS OF WOMEN IN YOUR CHURCH AND EXAMINE THE MINISTRIES THAT ARE ALREADY HAPPENING.

When Nehemiah arrived in Jerusalem, he strategically took a few men with him to examine the walls. He assessed the situation before he started rebuilding. I recently watched the 2016 movie, "The Founder." It's based on the story of Ray Kroc and his pursuit to change the fast-food industry by taking over a small and successful restaurant named McDonald's®. While Kroc's leadership style isn't one to emulate, the film captures Kroc's introduction to the McDonald brothers' new way of making hamburgers. After years of being in the food business, the McDonald brothers took careful consideration as to the process of food delivery. They "rebuilt the wall" of the food industry, streamlined production, introduced disposable wrappers, and sought a better way to do business.

In the same way, it's time to evaluate and assess the hows of your ministry. Ask yourself (and like Nehemiah, include a few others) these questions:

How would you describe your current ministry?

How would other women in your church describe your current ministry?

If you could describe what you want your ministry to be, what would it look like?

What obstacles stand in your way?

What things are currently working well? How can you build on those?

What's not working well? What needs to change, and how will you get there?

BUILDING BLOCKS FOR YOUR MINISTRY FROM NEHEMIAH

Nehemiah developed a strategic plan for rebuilding the wall. He understood the importance of gathering a team and delegating responsibilities, but he also developed a strategic plan.

NEHEMIAH 1–2	Ministry begins with prayer, purpose, and permission.
NEHEMIAH 2	Ministry needs vision but also execution.
NEHEMIAH 3	Ministry involves several people.
NEHEMIAH 4	Have an understanding that ministry often encounters opposition, and people get weary.
NEHEMIAH 5	Ministry may come with injustice and call for courage, but perseverance is necessary.
NEHEMIAH 6:15-16	Ministry should celebrate success and give God the glory.

DEVELOPING A PLAN

**Vision is the art of seeing things invisible.[3]
—Jonathan Swift**

For years, I have used a simple formula to develop purpose in ministering to women. I use three words that begin with the letter E. It's just "easier" for me.

ENCOURAGE

I believe ministering to women begins when we build courage into one another. Encouragement is infusing hope or courage into another's life. In the early church, people were sent to encourage believers in their new faith, to spur them on to be strong in the midst of persecution. First Thessalonians says,

> **Therefore encourage one another and build**
> **each other up as you are already doing.**
> **1 THESSALONIANS 5:11**

I don't know about you, but I think every woman needs encouragement. Whether they need encouragement in their relationships, in their work, or in the midst of their struggles, one of the most important aspects of ministering to women must be your desire to encourage them.

Drew Dudley delivered another one of my favorite TED Talks® entitled, "Everyday Leadership" in 2010. While you might be drawn to the title on leadership, his illustration of a lollipop was the "sticky" point of his presentation for me. He shares how the simple act of giving a young woman a lollipop and encouraging her through humor changed the trajectory of her life—and he didn't even remember the incident.[4]

Dudley says we've made leadership into something bigger than us, something beyond us. We've made it about changing the world and doing things that only a few people can accomplish, yet leaders are people who do things every day to encourage others.

EMBRACE

Whether you embrace someone in affection or you adopt an idea, there is a sense of intimacy and ownership. Your ministry should offer ways to help women seek Jesus Christ through His Word and through a personal relationship with Him. As a believer, you not only believe the doctrinal truths of repentance and salvation, but you draw close to God in an intimate relationship. He communicates through His written Word, and we cry out to Him through prayer. Our embrace of God should be so tight that we identify the Holy Spirit as the One who dwells within us.

Paul said in Acts 19,

> Did you receive the Holy Spirit when you believed?
> Did you take God into your mind only, or did you also
> embrace him with your heart? Did he get inside you?
>
> ACTS 19:2, THE MESSAGE

ECHO

I adopted this idea from a former women's leader who helped shape my thoughts of ministry. Women should embrace Christ, and in return they should echo His heart for the world. We accomplish this through the disciplines of sharing our faith and living on mission with God. Christian women must be obedient to pray for the lost and be radically involved in reaching the nations as well as our next-door neighbors. Our spiritual lives must create an echo that affects a much larger world than we will see. Just as an echo repeats a sound, we must repeat the teachings of Jesus through our daily actions. First Thessalonians 1 says,

> Your lives are echoing the Master's Word, not
> only in the provinces but all over the place. The news
> of your faith in God is out. We don't even have to say
> anything anymore—you're the message! People come up
> and tell us how you received us with open arms, how you
> deserted the dead idols of your old life so you could
> embrace and serve God, the true God.
>
> 1 THESSALONIANS 1:8-9, THE MESSAGE

You, too, must develop a plan for reaching women. Like Nehemiah, you might encounter opposition. You may grow weary in the process. But, if you persevere and seek the Lord's direction, you can develop a ministry that brings women to Christ and glory to God.

My desire is for the following pages to provide some new insight, new ideas, and new vision that you may implement in your local church ministry. These chapters are meant to encourage you on this incredible journey of ministering to women—not to make your name famous, but to make the Lord's name famous.

Let's get started.

CHAPTER 2

DEVELOPING A TEAM:

BECAUSE TOGETHER

EVERYONE ACHIEVES MORE

———

I have a competitive nature. I like winning. I may not be an elite athlete, or even a good athlete, but I love the thrill of winning a board game or the satisfaction of winning an argument. This competitive nature isn't always pretty. It's definitely a part of my personality that still needs sanctification. Even my past athletic experiences were often based on my own determination and perseverance. Whether I was running cross country or swimming in high school, the outcome and performance depended on me. I didn't play team sports, didn't like group projects, and oftentimes I enjoyed situations in which the thrill of victory or the agony of defeat rested solely on my shoulders. In short, winning came down to me, myself, and I.

Since then, I've learned this competitive nature and individualistic bent does not go far in ministry. I've learned that even when I've been tapped to be the "leader," I'm more successful when I'm not doing life alone. Ministry success has never come from my own hands but through the hands of many. I've learned the Lord directs ministry, but He uses people to accomplish His purposes—women with different personalities, spiritual gifts, passions, and life experiences.

> **Without guidance, a people will fall, but with
> many counselors there is deliverance.**
> PROVERBS 11:14

I also like the old saying, "Many hands make light work." In short, teams work. I originally heard the acronym TEAM—together everyone achieves more—when I began my first ministry assignment. My role was to develop student ministry leaders in our church, to prepare them to lead students, and to train them to lead Bible study. I knew quickly that reaching students for Christ took more than one personality or one big event. It took relationships and investment from adults who had hearts to serve students. I can still remember when my husband taught middle school boys on Sunday mornings. One of the young men from his class landed in the hospital after an accident. When he was asked if he had a youth minister, this eighth grader proceeded to name my husband and not our student ministry leader. Because our ministry wasn't based on the personality of one student minister, everyone on our team saw themselves as a minister. Our church philosophy of "every member is a minister" became more than a slogan. That teamwork mentality became part of our identity as a church. Developing a team is vital to the success of ministry, no matter where you serve.

Is your natural tendency to gather a team to do the work, or do you tend to try to shoulder the load alone? Explain.

Do you know why that's your natural inclination? Does that practice lead to healthy patterns for you and for the team that you're leading? Why or why not?

What aspect(s) of your ministry/work do you find most difficult to delegate or share with others? Why?

BUILDING A TEAM

Building teams isn't just practical. It's biblical. You don't have to look much further than the life of Jesus to see the importance placed on biblical community and teamwork. Jesus took the most unlikely group of men as His twelve disciples. They were tax collectors, fishermen, and political zealots with a variety of passions and life experiences. He lived life with them, taught them, confronted them, encouraged them, and gave them the challenge of taking the gospel to the world. An entire book could be written on the team Jesus built and, in fact, there are many works that look extensively at how Jesus built His team.

I'd like to examine the practicality of teams through the eyes of one of Scripture's most influential leaders—Moses. In Exodus 18, Moses' father-in-law, Jethro, paid Moses a visit. I love thinking about this scene because the son-in-law and father-in-law relationship can be an interesting one in today's culture. Most father-in-laws I know are watching out for their daughters. *Will this guy take care of my little girl? Will he provide? Will he love her and treasure her as much as I do?* Daddies want the best for their little girls—no matter how old they are.

I'm not sure how Jethro felt about Moses as his son-in-law, but I think Scripture describes a relationship that was honest and caring. One thing we know—Jethro was a new follower of Yahweh. His newfound faith combined with his former position as a Midianite priest gave Jethro a unique perspective on how Moses was operating. Jethro became a mentor to Moses when he realized that Moses had taken on too much of the workload. As Tony Merida describes in *Exalting Jesus in Exodus*:

> [Moses] was like the police, the law, the counselor, the department of motor vehicles, the judge, the theologian, and the pastor all in one. This task was too heavy.[1]

Read this account in Exodus 18. Do you often feel overwhelmed with ministry tasks?

In what ways do you feel like Moses?

How can you apply Jethro's principles to your current ministry assignment?

Jethro summed up the situation in verse 17, "What you're doing is not good." And in verse 18, Jethro continued, "You will certainly wear out both yourself and these people who are with you, because the task is too heavy for you. You can't do it alone." Boom. Mic drop. Reality hits. Jethro spoke honestly with Moses: You need others. You must share the ministry. Your job as a leader is to equip others for the work, just as Paul exhorted the Ephesians to equip the saints for the work of ministry in Ephesians 4:12. It doesn't mean you aren't carrying your load—you just carry the load that's meant for you. Additionally, Jethro didn't simply identify the problem. He provided a plan. I love what verse 19 says:

> Now listen to me; I will give you
> some advice, and God be with you.
> EXODUS 18:19a

Jethro encouraged Moses to divide the people into groups, with leaders of thousands, hundreds, fifties, and tens. Moses listened to the plan and executed it. He was no dummy—following Jethro's advice not only accomplished more but enabled Moses to do an even greater work and pursue the tasks and assignments God had specifically for him.

As the leader of this ministry, what do you think God is specifically calling you to do? Be as detailed as possible in your answer.

What obstacles keep you from solely carrying the load meant for you?

What concrete next steps could you take to practically move toward the freedom of carrying out the task God has meant for you?

Who could you raise up as leaders to take the other loads that you're shouldering now?

THE IMPORTANCE OF DEVELOPING TEAMS

Let's summarize the why for a moment and consider the importance of developing teams. First, teams bring people together with a common goal. Whether the goal is to organize a Bible study, an event, or a mission trip, teams rally around a common aim and destination.

Second, teams reflect the body of Christ and its diversity of gifts. When you include women with the gift of administration, service, giving, hospitality, teaching, and others, your team can build on its strengths to accomplish more. I always encourage ministry leaders to provide a variety of assessments to their teams. Lead them to take a spiritual gift assessment or discover their personalities and strengths through one of the many available tools. There are several options available for free online, or you can purchase a variety of assessments. (We've included a sample Spiritual Gifts Survey in the Nuts and Bolts chapter of this book.) These are not meant to be definitive predictors of people, but they are tools that will help you learn how to best utilize those who are on your team. I recently took an assessment that helped me identify my conflict management style—something important when working with different teams. Assessments are tools that give you general feedback on people's personalities, spiritual gifts, and the ways they relate to others. But they often don't account for experiences and passions. Use assessments wisely, but don't pigeon-hole people into certain tasks because their assessment scores are high in one area. For example, a woman might have the spiritual gift of hospitality, but that doesn't mean she should always be a greeter or bring food to Bible study.

> If someone says no, it doesn't mean it's forever. It just might mean it's not the right time in her life.

Don't exclude a woman's past experiences when considering how she can contribute to your team. Consider how you can use her experiences and expertise to provide significant contributions to your ministry. As Reggie Joiner, the executive director of Family Ministries for North Point Ministries, once said,

You can tell people they are significant, but until you give them something significant to do, they won't feel significant.[2]

Third, when you develop a team, or teams, you reach more women. If you look back at the example of Moses, Jethro suggested finding "commanders of thousands, hundreds, fifties, and tens" (Ex. 18:21). Too often we focus on finding commanders of many when we should concentrate on finding commanders of ten. Developing a leadership team trickles down to developing leaders of small groups who can multiply ministry in new ways. We need more leaders of ten than we need leaders of thousands.

Fourth, teams create a place for biblical community. I've experienced some of the sweetest moments of spiritual growth in my ministry in a team setting. Whether we were praying as one united group, playing games, or learning how to teach God's Word more accurately, teams become what the psalmist described in Proverbs:

> Iron sharpens iron, and one person sharpens another.
> PROVERBS 27:17

Don't forget to celebrate with your team— especially when they are volunteers.

When you rally around the common goal of reaching women with the gospel in the context of biblical community, your team will take ownership. They will see the goal as something from the Lord—something that has eternal value and visible, eternal fruit.

Now that we've covered the why of having a team, where do you start? How do you identify team members? What qualities do you want in your team? How do you enlist them? What expectations should you have for them? These are all important questions to ask. While the list might seem long and extensive, the most important thing you can do is begin right where we started—with prayer.

Take a few moments to sit with God and give Him all of your thoughts about your team. Ask Him to reveal direction, illuminate His Word in discerning His will for your ministry, show you the women He might be leading to your team, convict you of any sin in your own life, and realign any misperceptions in your heart and mind. Journal your thoughts or a prayer as you spend time with Him.

IDENTIFYING AND ENLISTING TEAMS

I love making lists. There is hardly a Monday morning when I don't begin my week making a long list of priorities: things to do, meetings to attend, and so forth. Making a weekly list became a habit for me right after college when my first boss required it. Each week I would literally write out my list, make a copy, and share it with my supervisor. It provided a framework for my week and the accountability to accomplish the most important tasks at hand.

My lists have changed a bit since those days. When I started leading ministry teams, there was one significant addition to my weekly list—the names of women I prayed about inviting to become part of a team. This prayerful habit is a weekly reminder to seek the Lord's direction about team members. I've learned the importance of praying for them. Over time I've come to seek certain qualities before asking someone to join. Here are a few of the qualities I consider when praying for potential team members.

QUALITIES TO LOOK FOR IN POTENTIAL TEAM MEMBERS

CALLED

Do they sense God calling them to join the team? Has God placed a desire in their hearts to serve? I'm not just looking for volunteers to fill a hole. I'm looking for servant leaders who understand that being part of a ministry team has spiritual significance.

CREATIVE AND VISION-CASTING

My task, as leader, is to bring creativity and vision, but I seek others who love thinking in new ways and can move us beyond the status quo.

ENCOURAGING

One of the primary tasks of your ministry is to encourage women. Others who are consistently looking for ways to cheer women on should champion your ministry.

EVANGELISTIC

Notice I didn't say they had to have the gift of evangelism— but women on your team do need to be burdened for others who don't know the Lord. These women are passionate about their faith and don't mind telling others why.

GRATEFUL

This goes both ways. As a leader of teams, I must show gratitude to those who serve, but I also want team members without an air of entitlement or privilege.

ORGANIZED

Not everyone will be a detailed person, and if they were, it would be disastrous. Yet, I look

> Even though someone may rotate off a team, find ways to keep her included and use her expertise.

for women who can manage their schedules, show up on time for meetings, and find time for preparation.

FAITHFUL, AVAILABLE, AND TEACHABLE

Some people love using the acronym for this—FAT. But, somehow, telling women they should be FAT doesn't always translate so well. Nevertheless, I want women on my team who are faithful to the Lord, faithful to their commitments, and faithful to the team. I look for team members who don't always know all the answers, but they're willing to learn and will put in the heavy lifting of being leaders who are learners.

HAS GREAT POTENTIAL

Popular pastor and author, Wayne Cordeiro, once told the story of a ministry leader who was complaining about having enough leaders. Cordeiro asked the leader to describe what he saw when looking at a forest. The man said, "'Elementary, Watson,' he quipped. 'Trees.' 'That's your problem,' I replied. 'All you see are trees. You've got to see more than trees. You've got to see the houses. When I look at a forest, I see houses, dressers, rocking chairs, bed frames, cabinets and desks. They're all in the forest. No, you won't find them already completed. But the potential is all there.'"[3]

SOWS UNITY

Just one look at Philippians 4 makes me break out in hives. When Paul admonishes Euodia and Syntyche to set aside their differences to further the gospel, I take seriously the need for unity among a team of women. I want women to seek reconciliation in all matters because Christ has called believers to be ministers of reconciliation, not just ministers to women.

How do you find leaders? Even if you're in a small church, it's no small task to discover potential leaders for ministry. You may feel like your pool is limited and there aren't many options. If this is you, take heart. You don't always have to look for leaders within the church. In fact, looking for leaders outside of the church walls can be a source of evangelism and church growth. If you meet a woman who is already leading outside the church, develop a relationship with her. Look for opportunities to have gospel conversations and invite her to be part of God's forever family. (By the way, this is a good idea no matter what size of congregation you are in!)

Another thing to consider when discovering leaders is to ask others for input. Remember, you don't always have a handle on all the relationships within your church, but collaboratively, you can discover other great leaders of whom you might not be aware. Ask church staff members. Ask the person who is in charge of new member classes. Ask the women currently serving on your team.

Seek a variety of women to serve on your team. Depending on the size of your leadership team (I would suggest no more than twelve), consider the ages and stages of life represented. Are there single women? Divorced? Senior adults? Young women? Women who work outside the home? Moms of young children? Empty nesters? You get the idea. You need diversity and variety—in ages, stages, races, and economic status. If your leadership team looks like a group of your best friends, it's likely your women's ministry will be a reflection of you and not the entire body of Christ. Instead, strive for a ministry that looks a little more like your entire church. You want a ministry that is as diverse as heaven will be.

CREATING A TEAM

How do you invite team members? Here are a few suggestions:

- **INTERVIEW POTENTIAL LEADERS.** Take them to coffee. Hear their hearts and begin to develop relationships with them. Hear their testimonies of coming to Christ and prayerfully invite them to join your team.

- **DEFINE ROLES AND EXPECTATIONS.** Women are busy, and they want to know what's expected of them. Write down your expectations, and send them a document. Try to be as specific as possible so they can prayer-fully consider whether they can fulfill the role you've asked of them. Some teams will have specific assignments, while others may be more general in their responsibilities. Either way, spell out what you'd like from them.

- **PROVIDE ASSESSMENTS ON SPIRITUAL GIFTS, LEADERSHIP STRENGTHS, AND PERSONALITIES.** We've already touched on this briefly, but if your women aren't sure about these things, give them the opportunity to discover more about themselves through assessment tools.

- **ASK THEM TO PRAY.** Give women ample time to seek the Lord, but also let them know when you need an answer. You might be surprised when some tell you that they've been praying about joining the team for a long time.

- **PROVIDE A TEAM COVENANT.** In the last chapter of this book, you'll find a sample covenant that you can use (p. 127). By providing a covenant, you are asking the women on your team to commit to the responsibilities and expectations you've already set before them. Give them an amount of time (usually a year) that you expect them to serve. After a year, you have the opportunity to evaluate whether they have kept their commitment and may continue on the team, or if they may need to step down.

- **ROTATE TEAMS.** On some teams, consistency for the long haul is important. These teams usually have very specific skill sets and require-ments. On the other hand, a general leadership team should implement a routine rotation to provide for the ongoing development of future leaders. Usually, I ask women to serve for a year, with a maximum of three years, before they rotate and give other women the opportunity to serve.

VARIOUS KINDS OF TEAMS

Depending on the size of your congregation and the breadth of your church's min-istry to women, there may be a need for several types of teams. While this list isn't exhaustive, here are a few ideas for types of teams your ministry may benefit from:

LEADERSHIP OR VISIONARY TEAM	Begin here when building a team. It consists of a combination of leaders from other teams or women who help you think about the overall direction you want to take. A leadership or vision team helps you think critically about where you've been and where you are headed in the future.
PROJECT OR EVENT TEAM	Focused on one specific area, for a finite amount of time, each of these teams has a concrete goal and specific task. For example, a retreat team works toward a project or event. Different people on the team take responsibility for various aspects of the project or event, such as registration, publicity, hospitality, food, and so forth.

DISCIPLESHIP TEAM	Concerned with getting women into God's Word, this team might be comprised of Bible study leaders (if you have more than one Bible study), small group leaders, or intentional discipleship group leadership.
PRAYER TEAM	Committed to making prayer a priority, these women pray for specific areas of your ministry to women. They might oversee a church-wide prayer ministry, lead prayerwalking in the community, or communicate prayer needs to a larger group of people within the congregation.
BENEVOLENCE OR NEW MEMBER TEAM	With a keen eye to see and meet the needs in your church, this team is responsible for helping with special needs, funerals, and meals for people in need. A new member team might find creative ways to welcome women into the church and seek to connect them to others. Depending on your context, you may need to divide these responsibilities into two separate teams.
GIRLS' MINISTRY TEAM	Aimed at creating unity among the generations, this team might work closely with the student ministry staff and seek ways to connect teen girls to the bigger picture of ministering to women. Whether they lead Bible studies for teen girls, oversee special events, or lead mission projects, there should be some intentionality in serving girls' needs and connecting different generations.
OUTREACH TEAM	Focused on reaching the world for Christ, this team is constantly looking for ways women can connect to the bigger picture of intentional investment in others. Their goal is to consistently provide opportunities for women in your ministry to have gospel conversations and meet needs in the community.
MISSIONS TEAM	Connected to the larger mission efforts of a congregation, this team may be comprised of women who lead in the efforts of mission giving and mission going, planning both local and global mission trips.
EMERGING LEADERSHIP TEAM	A small group of women who are in college and in their 20s, these young women can add creativity to your team, give new insight, and provide organic mentoring opportunities.

With your church context in mind, which types of teams do you need and what functions would they serve?

How might you take existing teams and restructure them for these purposes?

What are your next steps?

WHAT YOUR TEAM NEEDS FROM YOU

As a leader, you set the tone and you are the keeper of the culture for your team. The phrase attributed to Peter Drucker, "Culture eats strategy for breakfast" is true.[4] How do you develop a healthy team structure? Here are a few suggestions.

A TEAM ENVIRONMENT
Spend time with your team. Structure meetings so that everyone has an opportunity to participate. Focus on working collaboratively.

COMMUNICATION
Keep your team informed, whether it's through a weekly email, text messages, or face-to-face conversations. No one wants to be left in the dark.

ACCOUNTABILITY
The leader should be accountable to her team, but the team must also have accountability in regard to their responsibilities. Set them up for success by providing clear expectations, feedback, and encouragement.

CORRECTION
There are times when conflict will occur or expectations aren't met. As the leader, work through the process of peaceful reconciliation by meeting with team members one on one, praying with and for them, and loving them through the situation.

TEAM-BUILDING OPPORTUNITIES
Give your team opportunities to have fun, play, and get to know one another. Take them to new places. Include team-building games in

your meetings, and provide creative experiences to foster friendships.

RESOURCES AND LEADERSHIP DEVELOPMENT OPPORTUNITIES

Don't expect every team member to have the same knowledge about various aspects of ministry unless you are willing to give them resources that develop them as leaders. Whether it's providing a book or attending a conference, good teams grow together when they have the proper tools.

EVALUATION, CELEBRATION, AND RECOGNITION

These three areas are probably the most neglected in teamwork—but probably the most important. Teams must constantly evaluate their work, celebrate their wins, and recognize those who made significant contributions. For a moment, think about a great football team. Each week the team evaluates its performance from the past game and prepares for the next game. But after a great win, there is time for celebration. Players are awarded game balls or recognized as MVPs for their outstanding contributions. Now, how are you doing this with your ministry team? Are you evaluating progress? Are you celebrating when God does amazing things in your midst? Do you recognize team members who go the extra mile? Praise and recognition build loyalty within the team.

Now that you have an idea of what your team needs from you as the leader, which of these comes most naturally/easily to you? Which is most difficult?

Is there a woman on your team or a pastor/mentor in the area who excels in the leadership area that is most difficult for you? What might you learn and implement from their example as you grow in your leadership?

Develop trust within your team. Understand that conflict may be a pathway to greater things.

How are you celebrating wins with your team?

How can you incorporate these ideas at your next team meeting?

EFFECTIVE TEAM MEETINGS

I'm probably weird about this, but I love meetings. Let me rephrase that. I love meetings when they are planned, productive, and push people forward in the overall purpose of ministry. When leaders invest in the heavy work of preparing for a meeting, meetings are more fruitful, engaging, and can actually be something people look forward to.

How do you plan effective meetings? Here are some quick tips:

- **DEVELOP AN AGENDA, AND PLAN OUT YOUR TIME EFFECTIVELY.**
  If you've set aside an hour for a meeting, use your time wisely. Give everyone an outline of the meeting and know how much time you want to spend on each area. When women walk into the room, is there something that says you've thought about them? Have you provided something special? Do you have a resource waiting for them when they arrive? My first women's ministry leader always had an intentional yet small gift for every person on the team when we arrived. They were thoughtful, beautiful, and specific to the topic we planned to discuss. I always looked forward to her meetings because I knew she went the extra mile in advanced preparation.

- **BE ORGANIZED BUT FLEXIBLE.** Agendas keep you on time, but you also need to display flexibility. You might sense that you need to stop and pray during the meeting or you need to address an issue that wasn't planned. Be sensitive. As one of my favorite student ministers used to tell me, "Eat a flexi-cookie."

- **BEGIN YOUR MEETING WITH PRAYER AND FOCUS ON GOD'S WORD.** Ask one of your team members to lead a devotional time and have your prayer chairman prepared with a specific and intentional prayer time. For example, use a variety of prayer methods or emphasis at each meeting.

Large sticky notes are great tools to use in meetings!

- **PLAN MEETINGS IN ADVANCE SO WOMEN CAN PUT THEM ON THEIR CALENDARS—AND STICK TO THEM.** Finding a time to meet can be challenging, but if you're leading a team, give the women sufficient time to put the meeting on their calendars and stick to the plan. It's not impractical to look ahead six months so women can place dates on their calendars. Remember there is never a perfect time. Most likely there will be someone who can't attend. Things happen, but do your best to stick to your calendar plans.

- **ALLOW TIME FOR DISCUSSION AND COLLABORATION.** If the meeting only consists of you talking, then an email would suffice. Meetings are meant for group discussion—as a time for others to give input and direction. Be intentional in the way you provide avenues for discussion, either by dividing the team into smaller groups, using whiteboards, or supplying specific questions for dialogue.

- **CELEBRATE BY TELLING STORIES.** Stories are powerful and personal. Include them in your team meetings. Share the ways God is moving in the hearts of women and how He continues to provide. It's never a bad idea just to stop and say, "Thank You, God."

I'm a latecomer to the television show *The West Wing*, but it's been on my Netflix "continue watching" list for several months. As I watched an episode recently, I was reminded of the synergy and brilliance that results from an outstanding ensemble cast. I don't always know the real names of those in the show because the cleverness happens when there is good dialogue, seamless acting, and seemingly effortless collaboration. Whether it's the cast from *The Office*, *Downton Abbey*, or *The West Wing*, these television series succeeded because collectively the actors and actresses worked together as a team. When your ministry team works, you'll see the same kind of results—but with eternal value. Remember—you can do more together than you can do alone.

In light of all we've covered in this chapter, how is your team functioning?

Name two areas of strength and two areas in which you have room for growth.

As the leader, plot out the following to help you think about how you're going to improve in these areas.

FIRST STEPS

_____

_____

_____

_____

_____

_____

_____

_____

_____

SHORT-TERM GOAL

_____
_____
_____
_____
_____
_____
_____
_____
_____
_____
_____

LONG-TERM GOAL

_____
_____
_____
_____
_____
_____
_____
_____
_____
_____

MAKING DISCIPLES: THE HEART OF YOUR MINISTRY TO WOMEN

———

I have a distinct memory of finding my daughter's journal. She was in second grade, and I was attempting to clean her closet. I'm sure "good mothers" would have instructed their daughters to clean out their own messes, but Courtney tended to be somewhat of a hoarder. Making her part with anything created more tears than me secretly eliminating clutter with a large black garbage bag. I wasn't trying to snoop at her journal because, I thought, *What horrible secrets do most second graders have?* I opened her little notebook and found the sweetest second grade penmanship listing out of Bible verses. Beside each verse she wrote what she was learning from God's Word. I was floored. *Where did she learn this?* She had only been a Christian for a year, and she was journaling! In a later conversation with a friend, I mentioned my find. I was caught off guard when she told me, "Why are you surprised? Hasn't she seen you do the same thing? You've just been modeling it for her, and she's picked it up." Oh yeah. Maybe I was discipling my daughter and didn't even realize it.

Here's the deal. Whenever I begin a discussion on discipleship, it can go lots of directions and sometimes seem complicated. Discipleship was not meant to be that way. Basically, discipleship comes down to one simple question: are we helping people learn how to be more like Christ? Are we teaching women how to study God's Word? Are we teaching women more than just study skills? Are we showing them the power of God's Word to transform them? Are women's lives different because Scripture affects the decisions they make, the ways they prioritize their time, and the ways they impact others?

Disciple-making happens both intentionally and unintentionally. It starts with your personal desire to be a disciple of Christ. Robby Gallaty, pastor and author of *Growing Up: How to Be a Disciple Who Makes Disciples,* says, "In order to make disciples, we must first *be* disciples."[1] We can use the theological term sanctification, but to say it more simply, being a disciple is the lifelong process of determining to learn and grow spiritually. For example, as a young girl, I begged my parents to let me learn how to play the piano. I began learning simple notes, chords, and even how to play with both hands at the same time. It took multiple years of daily practice and instruction from seasoned teachers before I could play advanced pieces. I started playing "The Farmer in the Dell" in third grade, but by my senior year in high school, I was playing Beethoven's "Moonlight Sonata" from memory. Similarly, discipleship begins at the time someone becomes a believer and is a lifetime journey of daily instruction.

Consider your own discipleship journey for a moment. If you were raised in the local church, you probably began learning simple, concrete concepts about God's love along with elementary stories of the Bible. As you matured both physically and spiritually you graduated from concrete principles to more complicated applications of how Scripture transforms your life. If you were fortunate enough to have this upbringing, you most likely had instructors who taught you God's Word.

> Take a moment to consider your own discipleship journey, giving special attention to people and seasons of discipleship. Label instances of intentional discipleship and moments of unintentional discipleship.

> In your own discipleship journey now, do you enjoy the steady progression of growing and walking with God, or are you tempted to try to jump ahead?

> How does this show up in the lives of women to whom you are ministering?

How do you react to the fact that you may be unintentionally discipling others with the way you live? Is it challenging? Energizing? Explain.

You have women in your church who haven't been taught the Bible or who became Christ-followers later in life. Your ministry to women must step in and develop various discipleship opportunities for them. Bible studies, small groups, and consistent ways to get women into God's Word are not only vital but biblical. We must teach women how to hear, examine, apply, memorize, and meditate on Scripture's eternal truths. We must teach women to see the Bible as one whole story, to see the gospel implications throughout Scripture, and not only to read Scripture but be transformed by it.

Math may not be my best subject, but there is a math equation we must address when it comes to discipleship. Discipleship is a process of multiplication. The first person, outside of my parents, who intentionally discipled me was my first student minister, Mike Barnett. He took a handful of high school students, including me, and spent one summer teaching us how to have a quiet time, how to journal, and how to see God work through prayer. Mike was a college student that summer, and I still keep in touch with him. After graduating from college, he began a career of making disciples at a nearby health science center. For close to forty years, Mike has intentionally poured his life into making disciples who are preparing for the medical field. His disciples are all over the world, making an impact for Jesus in the healthcare industry. More importantly, his disciples have made disciples who have made disciples. His reach goes far beyond the Bible study groups he started, because he spiritually "grandfathered" multitudes. Every woman I've invested in can be traced back to the principles he taught me. He will never know all of the women I've discipled, but because he spent one summer teaching me, there has been a ripple effect that spreads the gospel from one generation to another.

Name some of the people who discipled (are discipling) you.
What made their influence so impactful in your life?

Name a few things you would emulate from their examples.

If you weren't discipled, what do you wish someone had told/taught you as a younger believer?

Discipleship begins with relationship—both with God and with other believers. Mothers are natural disciple-makers. Grandmothers are natural disciple-makers. It only takes a quick look at 2 Timothy 1:5 to see the spiritual influence Lois and Eunice had on young Timothy. Paul, while giving instructions to one of his most faithful disciples, remembered where Timothy got his "spiritual roots"—from a godly family heritage. Paul acknowledged the past, but he also instructed Timothy for the future when he said in 2 Timothy 2,

> **What you have heard from me in the presence**
> **of many witnesses, commit to faithful men**
> **who will be able to teach others also.**
>
> 2 TIMOTHY 2:2

Timothy was a student, or disciple, of Paul's, and Paul entrusted Timothy to pass his instruction to others.

So where do you start this process in your local church? How do you create an environment of discipleship for women? In the rest of this chapter we'll discuss some practical how-tos and ways you can provide opportunities for women to dive more deeply into God's Word.

STEPS TO STARTING A DISCIPLESHIP AND BIBLE STUDY MINISTRY TO WOMEN

- **BEGIN WITH PRAYER.** Of course, this is always a good place to start. Sincerely pray about the needs of the women in your church. Ask the Lord for direction as you seek to offer Bible study.

- **ASK FOR INPUT.** Ask women what they would like to study. Ask your church leadership for affirmation on what you offer. Do you need to begin with one

Bible study? Do you need to enlist someone to organize more than one? When is the best time to offer a study? Where is the best place to offer a study? Gather information and don't be discouraged if you find an assortment of answers. Look for commonalities and begin small. Remember, one group of five can be replicated with five groups that can be replicated with more.

- **CONSIDER CHILDCARE.** Will you offer a study that accommodates mothers with young children? Spend time assessing the needs and consider choosing a time when childcare is already in place. Qualified childcare can be costly, but it is necessary if this is your demographic.

- **CHOOSE A TIME AND A PLACE.** What works for your group? Do you offer an evening study? A daytime study? Do you meet at the church? A home? A local coffee shop? How does the study work into the life of your church calendar? Again, you are going to find a variety of answers—especially if your congregation is large—so start small, and ask the Lord to multiply.

- **CHOOSE A LEADER.** Who is qualified to lead a study? Who has the desire to invest time both in personal study and in meeting with others? Is this woman faithful and trustworthy? For more insight, see Qualifications for a Bible Study Leader on page 41.

- **CHOOSE A STUDY.** Will you go through a book of the Bible verse by verse? Will you purchase a study that has video teaching? How much time have you allotted for Bible study? How many weeks will it last? How much personal study is involved between group sessions?

- **EQUIP OTHERS TO LEAD DISCUSSION.** Help women understand how to develop relationships with others in their groups, how to encourage balanced discussion, and how to pray for one another.

- **LOOK FOR INVESTMENT OPPORTUNITIES.** Keep your eyes peeled for chances to develop and equip women to teach the Bible on their own. We often rely on the expertise of published Bible studies. There is nothing wrong with using Bible studies. I'm an advocate of them. But I also believe the local church must equip women to study Scripture on their own and learn how to utilize women within the local church who have the spiritual gift of teaching.

- **FIND UNIQUE WAYS TO PROMOTE BIBLE STUDIES.** We have included an entire chapter devoted to helping you think of ways to promote your ministry to women and communicate with the women in your church effectively. (See p. 64.) But remember, it's important that women know what is being offered and when. Plan in advance so women can make Bible study a priority.

- **FIND WAYS TO EXPAND YOUR BIBLE STUDY TO INCORPORATE ALL ASPECTS OF MINISTRY.** Of course, the goal is to get women into God's Word, but you should also consider how you might include prayer, outreach, fellowship, and ministry opportunities. One Bible study can accomplish all of these goals if you're intentional.

- **CONSIDER THE QUESTION, WHAT COMES NEXT?** When you finish a study, are women eager to jump into another study? Instead of creating a place with perpetual learners of God's Word, are you creating opportunities for women to start their own groups? Are you encouraging them to not just be disciples but to make disciples? Far too often, women's Bible studies consist of the same women who keep taking study after study and never move beyond the role of a learner. We are all lifelong learners of God's Word, but as we mature in the faith, we lead others. We should challenge our women to do the same.

- **FINALLY, TAKE TIME TO EVALUATE.** What worked? Did women gradually lose interest? What steps can you take to make Bible study better? Ask women for their feedback and encourage them to make Bible study a priority in their lives.

Consider a time when Bible study changed your life. Describe the situation.

What was different or new about that experience, and how can you create a similar experience for others in your own Bible study?

What do you see as the greatest need for your women?

Because discipleship is such a vast topic—and one so vital to your local church—this chapter includes several lists of things to consider on the subject of small groups and Bible study. As always, be a perpetual learner of God's Word, but work to become a perpetual multiplier, if you aren't already.

QUALIFICATIONS FOR A BIBLE STUDY LEADER

A WOMAN WHO desires to serve others and has the willingness to learn

A WOMAN WHO is committed to your local church and lovingly cares for others

A WOMAN WHO continues to grow in her personal relationship with the Lord and leads a life of integrity

A WOMAN WHO understands biblical principles and has a good grasp of Scripture. She doesn't have to be an expert, but she must be someone who is familiar with the Bible and knows how to find biblical answers to life's questions.

A WOMAN WHO spends time in personal Bible study, is faithful in her attendance to group Bible study, and invests in building relationships with her group

TASKS OF A BIBLE STUDY LEADER

A WOMAN WHO listens to others and leads discussion

A WOMAN WHO facilitates balanced discussion in a diverse group with an understanding of group dynamics

A WOMAN WHO plans discussion time wisely, keeping discussion moving and the conversation focused on Scripture

A WOMAN WHO addresses conflicts in a biblical manner and seeks unity among the group

A WOMAN WHO looks for others in her group who might be future small group leaders

CHOOSING A BIBLE STUDY

KNOW THE WOMEN IN YOUR GROUP.

Know their needs and their levels of spiritual maturity.

KNOW YOUR CHURCH CALENDAR AND THE CALENDAR SEASONS OF YOUR GROUP.

Normally, fall and spring are good times to begin studies. But don't neglect summer studies, especially if you have a group of teachers who don't normally have time for Bible study during the school year. Avoid studies that extend into busy calendar seasons such as Christmas or late spring when end-of-school activities are in full swing. Check your church calendar to avoid conflicts with big events or activities such as Vacation Bible School.

CHECK OUT YOUR OPTIONS.

Whether you look at available studies online or at a local Christian bookstore, spend time getting familiar with studies, authors, the amount of personal study per week, and even the length of teaching videos, if applicable. You may want to complete the study prior to offering it to a group—either with an online Bible study or working through the actual study on your own personal time.

CONSIDER LOGISTICS SUCH AS LOCATION AND THE LENGTH OF TIME YOU'VE ALLOCATED FOR THE STUDY.

If you choose a study with video teaching, make sure you have the proper equipment and know how to use it prior to the start of the study. If you're meeting in a public place, such as a coffee shop, consider a study that limits the required resources to something such as a book with discussion questions at the end of each chapter.

CONSIDER A VARIETY OF AUTHORS.

Often women get fixated on one particular Bible study author and don't want to deviate. Offer a variety of diverse authors so women have a balanced diet of Bible study approaches.

TIPS ON CREATING A GREAT BIBLE STUDY ATMOSPHERE

One of the greatest tasks of a Bible study leader is to facilitate dynamic discussion in an encouraging environment. Here are some quick tips for Bible study group leaders.

- **ENCOURAGE WOMEN TO VERBALIZE THEIR VIEWS AND FEELINGS.** Let group members know from the beginning that you want participants who will listen and be open to others while also providing confidentiality. Women should feel free to share what they've learned and how they're processing life struggles within the group.

- **BE GRATEFUL FOR EVERY ANSWER.** Affirm answers—even if they're wrong—by saying that you appreciate the input. If the answer is wrong or isn't what you were hoping to hear, encourage others to respond by asking them another question. You might say, "How did you come to that conclusion?" or "Did someone find something else?" In other words, help the group get to a better answer or the "right" answer. You don't want to shut a group member down because if you do, she'll likely be afraid to participate in discussion, and she may even stop attending your group.

- **DON'T BE SATISFIED WITH THE FIRST RESPONSE TO YOUR QUESTION.** Even if the first answer is a great answer, encourage others to add to the discussion. This is especially important for women in your group who are introverts or who need more time to process how they want to respond. Usually, these women have great input but need a little more encouragement and time to share.

- **KEEP THE DISCUSSION MOVING.** If you have thirty minutes for discussion and five days of material to cover, don't get bogged down on the first day. Watch your time, and keep the discussion moving. Before you meet, circle the most important questions that you want to make sure to discuss as a group, putting a number next to the question and a time. The number represents how many people you want to respond to the question, and the time will give you a reminder to stay on track.

- **BE ALERT TO THE INDIVIDUALS IN YOUR GROUP.** Watch the body language of others in your group, and be attentive to signs of those who might need your consideration. Watch for emotions, and be sensitive if the Holy Spirit prompts you to spend additional time with a particular woman.

- **DON'T BE AFRAID OF SILENCE.** Too often, group leaders quickly become uncomfortable when no one immediately jumps in with an answer to a question. Instead, use the silence as a time for group members to think more deeply about the question at hand. If silence continues, consider revising the question or restating it in another way, in case they misunderstood the first question. If you have a talker in the group who isn't normally afraid to answer, ask her to share if she has any insight. It may just take one person to start a bigger discussion.

- **TURN DIFFICULT QUESTIONS BACK TO THE GROUP.** More than likely, you, as the group leader, will be approached with a difficult question from a complex passage of Scripture. If you don't know the answer, ask others for input. If there's still uncertainty, tell the group that you're going to spend time looking for a better answer before you meet again and find the help you need to bring clarity to the question.

- **LET YOUR GROUP SELF-CORRECT ITS TANGENTS.** It's not unusual for a group to get sidetracked in the middle of a discussion, but normally someone will redirect the group back to the subject at hand. If not, don't be afraid to rein in side discussions and move to the next question.

- **STAY FLEXIBLE.** It's great to stay on task and finish every question you prepared. But be flexible if the group needs to "camp out" on a particular question or if a specific ministry need arises from the group during discussion. If you're flexible and attentive to the Spirit's guidance, you may be surprised at how God directs the conversation in a way you didn't see coming!

- **INCORPORATE FELLOWSHIP OUTSIDE OF THE SMALL GROUP TIME.** Some small groups will incorporate a time of fellowship within the study, but often there's a limited amount of time to complete the Bible study. Women will develop friendships and community within the group, but also intentionally look for opportunities to connect with each other outside the normal Bible study time.

- **LOOK FOR WAYS TO INVITE OTHERS WHO DON'T KNOW CHRIST.** Few women think of Bible study as a place to invite non-believers, yet it's the perfect place to let God's Word penetrate the heart of people seeking spiritual answers. Encourage your women to invite others, and make it a point during your group to pray for opportunities to share the gospel.

- **PROVIDE A LEARNING ENVIRONMENT.** Educators will tell you it's important to create an environment conducive to learning. Women need to have room to take notes and spread out with their Bibles, study books, and handouts. Circle configurations provide a natural environment for discussion and help eliminate the possibility of distractions.

- **CONSIDER OUTREACH ACTIVITIES AND MINISTRY PROJECTS.** Encourage your group to give toward a ministry project. Ask church leaders about projects that are already an ongoing part of your church's ministry, and look for creative ways to partner. These opportunities foster friendships and help group members look beyond themselves.

- **BE PREPARED TO LEARN FROM YOUR GROUP.** Creating a dynamic group atmosphere gives the leader an opportunity to personally learn new concepts and allows group members to gradually take on more responsibility and practice leading. It also prepares you as the leader for future opportunities to lead within the church.

- **ENCOURAGE WOMEN NOT SIMPLY TO STUDY GOD'S WORD BUT TO MEMORIZE IT.** Provide note cards and select specific verses from the study to learn together. Each week, encourage them to practice what they have memorized.

HOW TO MANAGE PRAYER TIME IN YOUR BIBLE STUDY

Spending time praying in your group is vitally important, but it can also lead to distractions, gossip, and insufficient time to complete your study discussion. Here are a few ways to better manage your prayer time during Bible study.

IT'S OK TO SET BOUNDARIES DURING PRAYER TIME.

Explain to the group that you have allotted a certain amount of time for prayer requests and actual prayer time. Setting a boundary will help ensure you're able to accomplish what you've prioritized.

BE CREATIVE IN THE WAYS YOU PRAY TOGETHER.

Some women are timid about praying together in a group, and many haven't prayed out loud, in front of others. Instead, find creative ways to allow everyone to participate. Assign each member a specific verse to pray out loud. Ask her to spend time in praise and speak out loud the names of God. (See p. 139 for a quick reference.) Spend time in thanksgiving, and have each woman share one thing for which she is grateful.

CONSIDER REQUESTS THAT RELATE TO THE PERSON IN THE GROUP, NOT DISTANT ACQUAIN-TANCES.

It's important to pray for your neighbor's step-brother who just had surgery, but when you may be limited for time, consider asking everyone to share prayer requests that are personally related to their needs or ways they can personally minister to someone else.

KEEP PRAYER TIME ON SPECIFIC REQUESTS, CAREFUL TO AVOID GOSSIP.

In line with setting boundaries, consider prayer requests that can be listed on a board in bullet form and shared quickly without a lot of explanation. When you see someone veering off into a conversation that leads to gossip, gently guide the person back to the request, and help keep the discussion moving.

INCLUDE SILENT PRAYER TIMES.

Lead everyone to share their requests, and then take a few minutes to silently pray for one another. Encourage women not only to take their requests to the Lord, but to allow the Holy Spirit to speak to their hearts.

MAINTAIN CONFIDENTI-ALITY.

Set this boundary from the beginning so women feel they can share their needs openly and without judgment. If a situation arises involving verbal/physical abuse or illegal activity, address the situation with church leadership. This may also involve contacting law enforcement officials and asking for guidance regarding next steps.

FIND VARIOUS WAYS FOR WOMEN TO PRAY TOGETHER.	You may not have time for each person in the group to pray. If that's the case, divide women into smaller groups of two or three, encouraging them to pray for one another and share requests within the smaller group. Vary your approach from week to week to keep it fresh.
PRAY IMMEDIATELY AS CONCERNS ARE VOICED, IF APPROPRIATE.	If a need arises in the middle of Bible study, don't be afraid to stop and pray immediately.
ENCOURAGE PRAYER FOR THE LOST.	Praying for those who have physical needs is important, but even more pressing is prayer for family and friends who need to come to Christ. Keep those requests in front of them and encourage your group to look for ways to not only pray for non-believers but for opportunities to share their faith with others.
KEEP A PRAYER JOURNAL FOR THE GROUP.	As a group leader, keep a small notebook of requests that people have shared. Check on specific needs throughout the next week and continue to pray for one another until God has answered the prayer. Encourage everyone in the group to keep a prayer journal so they can visually see how God has worked within the group over a period of time.

These tools are meant to be helpful handholds as you build Bible study groups, disciple women, and support the women in your ministry who are discipling others. But remember, ultimately you are striving to love these women well, point them to Christ, and walk alongside them in the ups and downs of their spiritual journeys. If a prayer time runs long or the dynamics of your Bible study aren't exactly as you'd envisioned, don't worry—you're all growing together. Be faithful, trust God, and He'll enable you to bear fruit.

> Take a few moments to brainstorm and dream. In your ideal scenario, what would discipleship look like in your ministry to women? List steps you can start in the next few months to develop your dream.

Pray for God to show you any pieces of that ideal that He wants you to work toward. Ask Him how you can best accomplish it.

CHAPTER 4

CONNECTING THE GENERATIONS: UNDERSTANDING THE WOMEN IN YOUR MINISTRY

Sue Ellen. Joyce. Millie. Donna. Wanda. Sherry. Deborah. Gwen. Esther. Martha. June. Willie. Ruby. Ann. Yvonne. Ann. Linda. Kathy.

Those names may mean nothing to you, but each of them represents a woman who has played a significant role in my life. Other than my mother, grandmothers, and the other Christian women in my family, the women of my church families have shaped the way I love my husband, the way I raised my children, and the way I've grown in my spiritual journey. A few of these women are in heaven, but I'm grateful to watch many of them finish their races proclaiming,

> I pursue as my goal the prize promised
> by God's heavenly call in Christ Jesus.
>
> PHILIPPIANS 3:14

One of the women who invested most significantly in my life was my Sunday School teacher during high school, Katherine Carter. I attended a church that ran an average of 350 on a typical Sunday, so it was normal to know women of all ages because everybody knew everybody. We didn't have to find ways to connect the generations; it just happened naturally. I remember that Mrs. Carter (because we never called a senior adult by her first name) showed up every week. She loved the Lord, and it showed in the way she spoke and the way she lived. She was humble and modest. I thought she was *the* model for godliness. Somehow, this 70-something, widowed pastor's wife connected her generation with my generation. I looked forward to each Sunday when Mrs. Carter opened her Bible, taught us timeless truths, and showed us that a life lived following Jesus was the greatest adventure we could ever hope for. She never went to camp and never went on a mission trip, but she was our high school girls' greatest advocate for following Jesus. I still smile when I think about the graduation gift she gave me—an orange nightgown that I'm sure was much more appropriate for a woman her age. Nevertheless, every time I wore it, it reminded me that she was an example of the godliness I wanted in my own life.

I never once questioned whether she was capable of being my teacher. I wasn't looking for a teacher who was young or fashionable. I wasn't looking for a teacher with a seminary degree. I just wanted to be in a Bible study with girls my age where we opened our Bibles and learned from the experience and wisdom of a woman who had lived a lot more life than us.

Maybe that class is why I love local church ministry. In today's culture, where young women want authors, speakers, and others who have a so-called platform (women with whom they'll likely never have a personal relationship) to mentor them, I think we've forgotten the simplicity of how local churches should be connecting the generations and providing natural mentoring opportunities. We've made mentoring a program, and we've forgotten that each of us will have multiple women to emulate in our lifetimes. The phrase "it takes a village" may also be said for connecting generations of women and being mentors for the next generation in the local church. The Bible's outline for mentoring says it best:

> **One generation will declare your works to**
> **the next and will proclaim your mighty acts.**
> PSALM 145:4

Declaring the works of God from one generation to another is a critical commandment of Scripture. The Book of Deuteronomy is filled with verses where Moses instructed the Israelites to teach the next generation, but none are more memorized or well-known than Deuteronomy 6:

> **Listen, Israel: The LORD our God, the LORD is one. Love the LORD**
> **your God with all your heart, with all your soul, and with all your**
> **strength. These words that I am giving you today are to be in**
> **your heart. Repeat them to your children. Talk about them when**
> **you sit in your house and when you walk along the road, when**
> **you lie down and when you get up. Bind them as a sign on your**
> **hand and let them be a symbol on your forehead. Write them**
> **on the doorposts of your house and on your city gates.**
> DEUTERONOMY 6:4-9

Known as the *Shema*, these verses were a declaration of faith, reminding Israel to keep God's Word front and center—literally. They also served as a reminder that a legacy of faith begins when you pass down the eternal principles of Scripture from one generation to another. Whether it was Moses mentoring Joshua, Naomi mentoring Ruth, Elizabeth mentoring Mary, or Paul mentoring Timothy, if one generation doesn't pass down its spiritual heritage to another, catastrophe and ungodliness follow. If you look at today's culture, it doesn't take long to realize that we've dropped the ball. We've become the epitome of Judges 21:

> In those days there was no king
> in Israel; everyone did whatever
> seemed right to him.
>
> JUDGES 21:25

Consider the people who mentored you. Take a moment to list them. We've included some different categories to help you brainstorm, but feel free to add your own as well.

Family:

Women in your church:

Women in history:

Authors and Bible study teachers:

Other:

I think that mentoring has to be Spirit-led and organic. Once when I was teaching a Bible study, I asked the women why they came. One of them said she was looking for a mentor. I just gave her my phone number, and she began to cry. I had no idea how much that meant to her. We've been close ever since, and that was more than six years ago. I've seen her mature and grow into a leader.
—Ginny

What hesitations to mentor do you see in yourself and the women you lead?

What do you need from a mentor?

What do you have to offer?

How can you help create a culture that fosters mentorship or godly relationships between women of all ages?

How can you show the women in your ministry what they have to offer?

So where do we begin? How can you make spiritual mothering a priority and not a program? It begins with the realization that all women have something to contribute. As Susan Hunt, author of *Spiritual Mothering* says,

> If you are a Christian woman who is seeking
> to grow in the faith and to live obediently,
> then you are qualified for spiritual mothering.[1]

She later adds,

> Being a spiritual mother means instilling Christ-confidence in a young woman so that she can leave [you] and face the world.[2]

I also like Esther Burroughs' definition of *mentoring* found in her book, *A Garden Path to Mentoring.* She says,

> Mentoring is making an emotional, spiritual, and physical deposit of seeds into someone's life to impact their season of life.[3]

In other words, if you're someone who desires both to grow in your faith and invest in the spiritual formation of others, then you can be a spiritual mother. If you're 70 years old or 25 years old, there's likely someone younger who needs you in her life. No matter how many candles you blow out on your next birthday, you're at an age to learn from someone ahead of you in life and be an example for younger women to follow. It's living out the biblical mentoring mandate of Titus 2:

> When someone wraps their arms around me with the love of Jesus and teaches me to be a better wife and mom— that is pure gold!
> —Amy

> In the same way, older women are to be reverent in behavior, not slanderers, not slaves to excessive drinking. They are to teach what is good, so that they may encourage the young women to love their husbands and to love their children, to be self-controlled, pure, workers at home, kind, and in submission to their husbands, so that God's word will not be slandered.
>
> TITUS 2:3-5

I believe one of the first things churches must do in order to cultivate mentoring relationships is convince older women they have something to offer a younger generation. Ask some older women to volunteer to serve as mentors and watch them scatter. Why? Because women's ministry programs have placed unrealistic expectations on the idea of being a mentor, and mentoring sounds like an intimidating task. Many Baby Boomers, for example, are active and young at heart. They see mentoring as a time commitment in a season of life when they possibly have other commitments such as caring for aging parents or helping with grandchildren. And they fear it might hamper their freedom to travel. They quickly recognize that adding another commitment seems idealistic—they aren't sure how they will be able to balance their current commitments with the addition of a mentoring relationship. Instead, let's consider a more realistic approach.

First, let's start with what a mentor needs. It begins with life experience. As I've already mentioned, if you've lived life longer than someone else, you have life experience to share with another woman. It also goes the other way. If you're younger, you have experiences and knowledge you can share with an older woman. Both generations benefit when there is a mutual exchange of learning from each other. When I was in college, I needed someone who had already lived a similar experience. I wanted to know what to expect when finals came around, how to navigate hunting for a job at graduation, and what dating should look like. Yet, life experience isn't enough. A godly mentor is a woman who has life experience and combines it with God's Word, prayer, and ministry opportunities.

In college, I found that combination in the life of Sherry. She was a senior in college when I was a freshman. She became my Bible study leader on Sunday mornings. Not only did Sherry care about me as a young woman, she cared about my spiritual growth. After college, she married and stayed in the same town, working as an elementary school teacher. A couple of years later, Sherry and her husband invited a group of students into their home at 6 a.m. on Thursday mornings for an entire school year. They taught us how to study the Bible, how to memorize Scripture, and how to share the gospel. When they moved to seminary, they encouraged each of us to start our own groups. At the age of 20, I was leading my first discipleship group. I'm sure I didn't know much, but Sherry's investment in my life shaped my heart to be a disciple who makes disciples. And guess what? Thirty-five years later, Sherry continues to disciple young women in the community where they serve at a seminary in Canada.

While mentoring may happen organically, there is some intentionality in being a spiritual mother.

This begins by understanding the various generations in your church. Many experts agree there are five living generations, the largest number of generations that have ever been alive at the same time in history. Current generations include the Silent/Greatest Generation (born 1945 or earlier), the Boomer Generation (born between 1946-1964), Generation X (born between 1965-1980), Millennials (born

> We should intentionally have friends from across the generations. When we build those relationships with younger women we become more solid in our own faith.
> —Kristy

between 1981-1996), and Generation Z (born 1997 and later).[4] It's important to know the history of each generation because those events shape the worldview and the way each group relates to others. While it's difficult to put everyone in the "box" of their generation, ministry leaders may find that learning about each generation provides understanding and can create paths of connectedness. At the end of the chapter (p. 60), you'll find some basic information about the three generations that currently most impact your ministry—the Boomers, Gen X, and Millennials. Take some time to understand what each generation has experienced.

Besides deeper understanding of the generations, working intentionally means knowing what younger women want from a mentoring relationship. Instead of "telling" a younger woman how to live, show her, love her, guide her, and work alongside her. This same pattern was present in Jesus' earthly life and ministry. Just as a gardener works intentionally in soil, you have the opportunity to cultivate the soil of a younger woman's heart. As you love her and guide her in God's Word, you will then find moments to nurture her into maturity.

You must also trust in the Lord who produces the fruit of mentoring relationships. As John 15 reminds us,

> Remain in me, and I in you. Just as a branch
> is unable to produce fruit by itself unless it remains
> on the vine, neither can you unless you remain in me.
> JOHN 15:4

Pray for a harvest of fruit from your relationships, but trust the Master Gardener to multiply the seeds.

Where do you begin in this process? Start by loving younger women and making yourself available to them. As the old saying goes, "People don't care how much

There is pressure for younger women to find the perfect mentor. We have to be careful that both come to the table without unrealistic expectations of each other. Some women have mentored me without formally knowing they were. It can look so different in various seasons of life.
—Heather

you know until they know how much you care." If you need help identifying a younger woman, begin with prayer. Pray for God to put on your heart a few young women you want to spend time with, and then ask them. Invite them to join you in your daily life—whether in your home, at church, or on the go. Show younger women how to be godly, yet be transparent about your struggles. Guide them to God's Word over teachable moments that happen both in structured and unstructured times. Connect Scripture to life, and share how God's Word has helped you, comforted you, and been your compass in every season. Find ways to work alongside them, and ask them to join you in the midst of your daily routine or vice versa. Invite them into your life and home, and remember your life doesn't need to appear perfect. It's about spending time together and not about whether your home is spotless.

Take a few moments to prayerfully consider younger women God might be prompting you to care for and mentor. Journal your thoughts here—make sure to include the names of the women to whom you feel God may be leading you.

PRACTICAL WAYS TO FOSTER MENTORING IN YOUR LOCAL CHURCH

Of course mentoring happens in the one-on-one relationships outside of your local church, but how can you foster relationships and connect the generations within the local church? Here are a few suggestions:

Begin with Bible studies.

If you have women's Bible studies, create opportunities for discussion between generations. Mix ages in your small groups, and enlist all generations to be part of the leadership. Encourage various ages to share with the entire group as a testimony to how God is using the study in their own lives. Finally, at least once, share a meal before or after your study as a way to encourage conversations beyond Bible study.

Ministry projects and mission trips are another way to foster mentoring relationships.

As various ages work with each other, you'll begin to see natural interactions happen. Whether it's serving a meal at a local shelter, learning a skill, or traveling together, these are some of the ways older women can connect with younger women as they work alongside each other. When my daughter was 14, I took her on her first international mission trip. We spent a week sharing a guest room with two senior adult women. I know my daughter got to see a new side of Miss Millie and Miss Jan as she watched them serve the Lord in a new context. She got to see their hearts for sharing the gospel in rural villages. Those kinds of experiences last a lifetime and into eternity as well.

Consider the types of events you offer women.

How are you incorporating multiple generations in your events? Start by including different generations in the planning team. Ask for everyone's input, allow younger women to lead certain aspects—and then *let them lead*! Provide opportunities for interaction during the event so women get to know new people. Connect women by giving them opportunities to share life skills or pray for one another. Deliberately plan events for different generations—such as an event for widows that allows younger women to serve and plan the event.

Creatively look for ways to connect the generations through prayer.

Encourage various ages to prayerwalk in your community. If you have Sunday morning classes divided by ages, connect an older women's class with a younger women's class by exchanging prayer requests. Prayer not only connects us with our Creator but with one another.

> Considering your ministry context, which of the ways to foster mentorship mentioned above would work best in your church?

> Can you think of other ways to foster mentorship?

MOMMIES, MENTORS, AND MCDONALD'S

Several years ago when I was leading the women's ministry in my local church, I knew we were missing a mentoring component. Discouraged by programs that required a lot of maintenance and coordination, I invited a small group of young moms to join me for a collaborative meeting. (I didn't call it a meeting—just coffee, bagels, and a hidden agenda.) I presented the concern—how were we connecting them to mentoring relationships, and how could our church foster these types of relationships?

So often we want to create a formula, and truly it is just doing life together.
—Candace

Within two hours, this small group of moms came up with an eight-week idea called Mommies, Mentors, and McDonald's. They chose eight subjects they wanted to learn from older women. These subjects ranged from how to have a quiet time when you have young children, how to cultivate your marriage, how to prepare nutritious and quick meals, and how to raise boys and girls. For each subject, they identified three women from our church they wanted to hear from. They determined hearing from three mentors instead of just one would give everyone someone with whom they could personally identify. And McDonald's? I challenged them to think beyond themselves and discover a way to invite other moms who didn't attend our church. The solution? After the session, the moms went to a nearby McDonald's for lunch and let their children have time together on the playground. I designed some inexpensive business cards with information about the mentoring sessions, and these moms connected with other moms and invited them to attend. The result? More than eighty women (and a bazillion children) attended our Mommies, Mentors, and McDonald's class during those eight weeks. Each week, these women learned from others, developed relationships with each other, and got to know the older women who had more life experience. The relationships formed in those eight weeks allowed a time of life-on-life learning while experiencing mentoring up close and personal. When we don't make these connections in the local church, the lost art of learning from one another can be as tragic as the story of Antonio Stradivari.

Antonio Stradivari is considered the premiere violinmaker ever to have lived. During his lifetime, primarily in the 17th century, he crafted close to 1,000 violins. There are approximately 650 identified Stradivarius violins still in existence and their craftsmanship is unparalleled.[5] As a possible pupil of Nicolò Amati, Stradivari learned his methods and developed his own, unique instrument. Stradivari violins are believed to be the best in the world, yet no one has been able to replicate them. Even though history shows Stradivari's son Francesco learned from him, his craftsmanship has not been replicated.[6] To purchase one of the remaining Stradivarius violins costs millions. This lost art is the consequence of one generation failing to learn from the master. As believers, your call to mentor and mold the next generation is not just a fun program for local churches; it's a biblical mandate. Take to heart the words of Psalm 78:

> We will not hide them from their children, but will tell
> a future generation the praiseworthy acts of the LORD,
> his might, and the wondrous works he has performed. ...
> so that a future generation—children yet to be born—
> might know. They were to rise and tell their children so
> that they might put their confidence in God and not
> forget God's works, but keep his commands.
>
> PSALM 78:4,6-7

When I think about my mentors, they are usually women who took the time to listen to my fears and continued to point me to Jesus.
—Holly

Don't allow the craftsmanship of our Creator to be lost on the next generation. Don't let the next generation fail to learn from your life. The cost is too great.

Take a few moments to consider prayerfully what God might be asking you to teach the next generation. Are there areas that seem too costly? Explain.

What holds you back? What spurs you on in telling the next generation about what God has done and is doing?

UNDERSTANDING THE THREE BIGGEST GENERATIONS IN YOUR CURRENT MINISTRY TO WOMEN

It's important to understand who your ministry is reaching and each generations' particular needs. The following information has been compiled by Chris Forbes, Alan Muehlenweg, and Kerry Bural in their book, *Hidden Harvest: Discovering Oklahoma's Unchurched.*[7]

BABY BOOMERS

WHO ARE THEY

In 1946, approximately nine months after World War II ended, the United States saw a "boom" in birthrates: 3.4 million babies were born that year, followed by 3.8 million in 1947. They account for approximately 30 percent of our current population, with 10,000 either retiring each day or reaching the age of retirement. This generation is often split into two cohorts: those born between 1946-1955 and 1956-1964 because of technological and cultural changes. Approximately 78 percent of them identify themselves as Christian.

KEYS TO UNDERSTANDING THEM

- They value individual choice and independence.
- They seek opportunities for community involvement.
- They tend to express issues in right-versus-wrong and divide people into good-versus-bad.
- They spearheaded the "counterculture" as young people, and now lead the "culture wars."
- They are a wealthy, prosperous generation and are often credited with establishing the American precedent for consumerism.
- They respond quickly to perceived injustices and will seek to right them.

TIPS FOR RELATING TO BOOMERS

- Clearly state objectives and goals to help them envision their roles.
- Present new and novel approaches without sacrificing tradition.
- Provide opportunities for them to take responsibility and demonstrate their passion and knowledge.
- Recognize their life experiences, and give them opportunities to share and teach from their own self-defining moments.
- Recognize their impact on younger generations, but offer opportunities to learn from younger generations as well.
- Provide opportunities for them to reflect on their youth; nostalgia can be energizing.
- Organize conferences and large gatherings; they tend to be highly motivated when initiating change as part of a large, influential group.

GEN X

WHO ARE THEY

Born between 1965 and 1980, they make up approximately 27 percent of the adult population. Approximately 70 percent in this generation identifies themselves as Christian. Gen X came of age in an era of failing systems and a disintegrating family unit. Born in the shadow of Baby Boomers, they were saddled with social problems that followed the civil unrest and over-consumption of the 1960s through the 1980s. Topics such as violent crime, environmental destruction, homelessness, high rates of teen pregnancy and suicide, corrupt politics, the AIDS epidemic, rising divorce rates, and dual-working parents are all identified in this generation. Even so, it is the first generation with a greater share of women than men graduating from college and moving forward in careers and additional education. They are frequently commended for their entrepreneurial skills.

KEYS TO UNDER-STANDING THEM

- As the first latchkey kids, they value self-reliance and independence.
- They tend to be skeptical of institutions and marketing ploys.
- They are entrepreneurs and support small businesses and individual efforts.
- They were introspective as youth but are now looking for opportunities to re-engage.
- They embrace diversity.
- They are highly adaptable to change.

TIPS FOR RELATING TO GEN X

- Above all, be genuine. They don't want to be manipulated.
- Recognize and leverage their abilities to develop new initiatives.
- They are a visual generation; find ways to deliver with compelling imagery.
- Offer opportunities for them to connect online and via email.
- When seeking their involvement in a project, provide the information they need to succeed and then let them handle the project.
- Offer opportunities for them to have a global impact.

MILLENNIALS

WHO ARE THEY

Born between 1981 and 1996, they are now approaching their late 20s and 30s. They represent approximately 30 percent of the adult population and 56 percent identify as Christian. They are one of the most talked about generations. Some have labeled them the "Boomerang Generation" or the "Peter Pan Generation" due to the perceived tendency for delaying some rites of adult passage such as marriage and career. This generation's size is not because of birth rates but because of immigration, which makes them the most racially- and ethnically-diverse generation in the history of the United States. They are generally confident, self-expressive, upbeat, and open to change. They are detached from politics and religion but highly connected through social media. They have grown up seeing bombings, school shootings, and watched the Twin Towers fall in New York City. Student loans plague this generation, causing many of them to put education on hold.

KEYS TO UNDER-STANDING THEM

- They value self-expression and have the tools to show it.
- Individuals to whom they can personally relate are a great source of inspiration.
- They are on track to be the most highly-educated generation in U.S. history despite student loan debt.
- They are motivated by authenticity.
- They are the least religious generation in modern times.
- They are committed to social justice and are tolerant of differing ideas and lifestyles.

TIPS FOR RELATING TO MILLENNIALS

- Start an authentic dialogue about what they're looking for and what they can contribute to a faith community.
- Increase efforts to combat social justice problems and provide opportunities for them to engage.
- Leverage social media to share events, testimonies, and ideas.
- Communicate openly and often about key issues, and solicit their feedback.
- Highlight causes, rather than institutions, and give them opportunities to be involved.
- When pursuing evangelical or community service opportunities, pursue active support of the local community, as well as the global community.
- Recognize and request their contributions; Millennials respect all generations and look for opportunities to learn from others, regardless of age.

COMMUNICATION: CAN YOU HEAR ME NOW?

As a women's ministry director, I often struggled to communicate what was happening in our ministry to women. Our church had multiple ministries and ongoing activities, and few announcements were made from the stage. Even if someone mentioned our next Bible study, it was often lost on the ears of a congregation more concerned about post-service lunch plans. Fortunately, in one fateful instance, creativity took over, and I devised a plan that would leave a lasting impression on our congregation.

We were entering a summer Bible study scheduled to meet in homes for eight weeks. I discovered an easy study based on the old television series, "I Love Lucy." (Disclaimer: I don't endorse the study, but it was appropriate for what we wanted to accomplish that summer.) The purpose was clear—we wanted to develop small groups in homes where women could attend one session or all of the sessions. We wanted to attract women who didn't attend our regular studies and weren't members of our church. We looked for something that didn't require personal study time. We secured all of the homes, and I pulled the leaders together to ask one simple question, "How do we get women in our church excited about this summer study?" We came up with several ideas to invite neighbors, but the most memorable promotion of the study took an unexpected turn. Instead of using normal communication processes, we purchased red wigs that resembled Lucille Ball's iconic hairstyle. On the Sunday prior to the beginning of the study, we all dressed alike and served as greeters when people entered the worship center. While we looked hilarious, we made sure every woman who attended our service got a personal invitation, including a postcard with details. Needless to say, our promotion of that Bible study was effective and memorable. More than one hundred women attended a study that summer, and many of them had never participated in a Bible study.

While this may not be the answer to getting the word out in your church, promotion and communication are extremely important if you want your ministry to be effective. Not only will you need to be creative, but you will also need to be intentional in the ways you invite women to the activities you plan.

Consider the bookends of your day—your morning routine and your bedtime routine. How often do you check emails and social media early in the day? How many nights a week do you check them one final time before you go to sleep? In today's culture, communication channels are crowded and diverse. You won't be successful if you aren't willing to go beyond the church bulletin, or worse, the church bulletin board. If you want to reach multiple generations, you need to explore many avenues of promoting and attracting the women both inside your church walls and extending the invitation to women in your community.

If you think the Bible doesn't show a clear-cut example of someone who had a message to communicate, think again. The whole of the Bible is God's communication to each of us! It's His message if we're willing hearers. It's His message for each of us to share.

In fact, in many instances God sent a messenger to provide information that needed to be communicated. He gave the prophets in the Old Testament specific messages for the Israelites. He appointed angels to deliver the announcement of Christ's birth. He commissioned people to spread the message of the gospel and the resurrection of Christ in the early church. One great example is found in 1 Thessalonians:

> Do you know that all over the provinces of both Macedonia and Achaia believers look up to you? The word has gotten around. Your lives are echoing the Master's Word, not only in the provinces but all over the place. The news of your faith in God is out. We don't even have to say anything anymore—*you're* the message! People come up and tell us how you received us with open arms, how you deserted the dead idols of your old life so you could embrace and serve God, the true God. They marvel at how expectantly you await the arrival of his Son, whom he raised from the dead—Jesus, who rescued us from certain doom.
>
> 1 THESSALONIANS 1:7-10, THE MESSAGE

You and I have the same mandate to declare the message of Christ through our ministry to women. So how are you echoing your news?

What has proven to be the most effective mode of communication in your ministry?

Who do you tend to reach most successfully?

Who do you struggle to reach?

Considering communication in your ministry, gauge how you're doing on a scale of 1 to 10.

Communicating well,   Struggling to communicate
communicating often   and doing so infrequently

1   2   3   4   5   6   7   8   9   10

In what ways can you be more creative in your approach to communicating your ministry?

Where do you begin? How do you make the most of communication? How do you communicate purposefully in what you say? Let's consider seven powerful ways you can be heard—and I promise they won't include wearing a red wig.

THE POWER OF INFLUENCE AND PERSONAL INVITATION

No matter where I hold an event, I always ask participants on post-event evaluations, "How did you hear about this event?" Consistently, the number one answer: one woman invited another woman. Sometimes women attend at the encouragement of someone on their staff, but most often, they don't want to come alone. If women like to go to the bathroom in groups, it only stands to reason they want to know they'll have someone else they recognize when they walk through the door of your next Bible study, event, or ministry activity. It takes just one person inviting another person to make a difference in the excitement and momentum of your next endeavor. A friend of mine was once discouraged because she wanted fifty women from her church to attend a bigger arena event that drew thousands of women, but only ten signed up. As she complained to her mentor about the disappointing results, the mentor commented, "But you have ten! Build on that." She found encouragement in knowing that if the weekend impacted ten women, they would return, tell their friends, and the group would grow the following year. She learned the power of a personal invitation—reaching a few and watching that number grow.

How can you encourage women to extend a personal invitation? Offer a "buy one, get one free" incentive if a woman brings an unchurched friend. Create announcements that can be shared in small groups or in Sunday morning groups. Enlist women from various age groups to be ambassadors for each group and disseminate information throughout the entire congregation. Above all, stress the importance of the personal invitation in your communication. The phrase, "who are you bringing?" may serve as a powerful reminder that no one wants to be left out. If you've ever wanted an invitation to be part of the "cool table," here's your opportunity to create one.

THE POWER OF EXISTING CHURCH COMMUNICATION CHANNELS

Most women who are leading studies or planning events in the local church are volunteers, which means they may not have an "inside" view of the existing communication channels at their church. Yet, someone in your church stands as the gatekeeper of communication. More often than not, that gatekeeper is a woman, so connect with her, and learn the ins and outs of how to get your message out there. Be her friend, and be grateful for the ways she promotes your activities. (A thank-you gift is never a bad idea!) Learn how far in advance information is needed. Write announcements the way you want others to share them, and offer a variety of ideas for communicating the message. Give the communications gatekeeper as much information as you can, because it will likely be edited. Usual church communication channels include the worship guide, e-newsletter, Sunday morning announcements, images on screens, and various signage placed around the church. Consider creative placement of your event or Bible study by placing posters on the backs of bathroom stalls or attaching them to the sinks in bathrooms. Ask for a kiosk or table in the foyer (if this is an option at your church), and have a sign-up table with more information. Find eager leaders who aren't afraid to talk to women as they pass by. They may provide that personal invitation we just discussed.

Develop a database of email addresses or contact information for women, and find an online service that will help you generate professional e-blasts. Again, your church may have something in place, so make sure you ask if you can use it. While some people might think emails aren't as effective as they once were, I disagree. Emails are sent directly to a person. She can read them, ignore them, or delete them.

In any case, she has to make a decision about whether to engage. It's your job to give her the information. (Remember, always provide a way for people to unsubscribe, and always gain permission to use their emails for your intended purposes.)

THE POWER OF SOCIAL MEDIA AND STORYTELLING

It's no secret that social media has consumed our current culture. While it can be a powerful way to spread bad news, it also provides a wide-open opportunity to spread your message and the gospel message.

It's dangerous to include statistics about social media because they become quickly dated, but in today's global population of 7.6 billion people, there are currently 3.196 billion active social media users. As of the date of this writing, the top social media outlets are Facebook (more than 2 billion monthly users), Instagram (800 million monthly users), and Twitter (330 million monthly users). In addition, YouTube boasts more than 1.5 billion monthly users.[1] Those are some pretty hefty numbers, so how do you make the most of your message through social media? Here are a few suggestions:

Engage in the "Big Three"—Facebook, Instagram, and Twitter.
Craft messages that not only promote your ministry to women, but inspire them to get into God's Word.

Use professional images, but don't steal them.
If you want people to see your message, use images that grab the viewer's attention. You can easily purchase these online. In fact, your church may already have a subscription used to secure stock photos. Check and see if you might benefit from those already available resources. Or, why not use real photos of your women? This creative idea makes your promotion more personal and often results in greater engagement and ownership from the women in your ministry. But, make sure to secure permission to use the picture before publishing it. Also be aware that using women from your congregation may pose an issue in the future if they leave your church or become divisive members of your congregation. (See the Appendix on p. 139 for social media app suggestions.)

Be authentic, and focus on the relationships between women in your group.
Don't just make a sales pitch. We were created for genuine relationships with others, and your ministry won't thrive without investing time in authentic connection.

Plan and be purposeful.

Have a social media mission statement, and set boundaries for what people can share and how often you will share. Use Philippians 4:8 as a starting point:

> Finally brothers and sisters, whatever is true, whatever is honorable, whatever is just, whatever is pure, whatever is lovely, whatever is commendable—if there is any moral excellence and if there is anything praiseworthy—dwell on these things.
>
> PHILIPPIANS 4:8

Embrace social media as a mission field through which others may share what is happening at your church.

Encourage women, especially your leadership team, to share posts and upcoming events. If you're promoting a Bible study, check the author or publisher's website for free promotional materials—many times you'll find free images or videos that you can easily share on all social media platforms.

Tell a story, don't simply pass along information.

Create a short video of a woman whose life your ministry has impacted. Give others a question, theme, or Scripture, and ask them to share their responses by recording them on video and uploading them to your social media site. And remember, keep them short! Most social media sites have time limits on videos.

Authenticity is more important than professional quality when creating videos on social media.

People want to see the "real you" and hear your heart. Be yourself. Don't over-edit. If you stumble on your words, that's OK! People want to feel like they know you more than anything else. You may also consider including two or three women in social media video posts, preferably friends who have fun together. Their warmth and friendship will be unmistakable and make other women want to join in on the excitement.

Minimize "insider" language.

Remember, you want everyone to hear and understand your message because you're sowing seeds in your social media mission field. For instance, if you desire to reach women outside of your church, they may not understand the terms "biblical community," "life group," or "flock leader." Always choose clarity over creativity.

Use hashtags.

Create a hashtag for your event, upcoming study, or ministry activity. Ask people to use the hashtag when they post on social media. This allows you and others to follow that particular event.

Remember, the Internet is permanent.

Think before you post, and seek advice from others to make sure your message communicates your intended idea. Even if there is a "delete" button, many a ministry leader has been left red-faced over something posted inadvertently.

Consider purchasing social media advertising if you want a larger audience.

The appropriate platform and message will depend on what you want to promote. But social media advertising is generally inexpensive and allows you to create specific target markets.

THE POWER OF CREATIVITY AND MAKING MEMORABLE MOMENTS

Gather your leadership team along with some of your most creative women, and think outside the box when it comes to promoting your next ministry activity. Our Lucy wigs made quite a memorable moment. If there's a theme you can incorporate, look for ways to instill your message. If there's a color you want to emphasize, make sure all your promotional materials match. Be consistent with your "look and feel" in branding for your ministry and specific events so that every time a woman sees your message she'll be reminded of your ministry.

THE BEGINNER'S GUIDE TO HASHTAGS

Not sure how to use a hashtag? Not sure what a hashtag is? Hashtags are short links preceded by the pound sign (#). Using them allows you to organize content and track keywords from other social media users. You can join a larger conversation when you use a hashtag that connects one subject together. It's commonly used with Twitter and Instagram platforms.

DO
- Use hashtags to form a community, to start a movement, to advertise an event, and to organize comments.
- Choose something that's easy, short, and unique to your event (as much as possible).
- Stick with it. Print it out for people. Promote on screens if you have screens.
- Use it yourself on Instagram and Twitter.
- Check the hashtag and like, repost, and comment on others' posts using a hashtag. (LifeWay Women uses the hashtag in most studies and event posts on Instagram and Twitter. You can steal our stuff! We love when people do that.)

DON'T
- Use spaces in hashtags.
- Use punctuation marks.
- Use different symbols such as the @ sign. The @ directly communicates to a social media user, not a topic.

Consider using different senses when promoting your ministry. Most of the time, promotion involves sight or sound, but there may be something you can incorporate that involves touch, taste, or smell.

For instance, you might treat women to a food item that connects with what you are promoting. Make cookies with the theme of your next event and distribute them on Sunday morning. Make small bags of trail mix to promote a camping theme or distribute take-home s'more kits. Consider a creative, hands-on approach to your next event. One time I led a retreat with a superhero theme. We distributed handmade capes to group leaders and asked them to create unique superhero capes that represented their groups. The group leaders wore them at the retreat—I only wish I had given prizes for imagination!

Never skimp on the creativity of a printed piece. Find resources to ensure you have professional artwork, and find new ways to distribute the information. I've told many leaders that if you want to attract younger women, use art that attracts younger women. Older women don't mind "young art." They see it every day in magazines and on television. Elevate your printed pieces so they aren't just informative but informational in a way that attracts others. Consider clever ways to get your information to women at your church. Distribute information in diaper bags, in small groups, in the lobby area of your church, and any place women gather.

THE POWER OF REPETITION

How many times do people have to see your promotional message before they really see it once? Some people say it takes seven times before people hear your message. It may be more today because attention spans seem to be getting shorter and shorter. In any case, this means you must repeat your message over and over again—and in different ways. Here are eight different ways you can promote your message to make sure your method doesn't feel stale:

1. Worship Guide and Video screens

2. Mass text messaging promotion

3. E-newsletter

4. Social media

5. Facebook Live video

6. Poster displayed in a bathroom

7. Information table in the foyer

8. Verbal announcements

These are just the easy ways to promote your message! So get creative, and get your message out over and over.

> **Consider your last women's activity. Did you incorporate a variety of methods and messages in regard to communication? If so, how?**

> **What could you have added or done differently?**

THE POWER OF LISTENING AND EVALUATING

Communicating your ministry activities starts on the front end, but you still have work to do on the back end. Any ministry activity begins with listening and ends with evaluation. Before you begin planning your next study, event, or ministry activity, listen to the needs of your women. Ask questions. Provide a survey (see example in the Nuts and Bolts chapter on p. 120). Create listening groups, and get feedback from others. Create an environment of buy-in at the beginning so there is a sense of excitement before you ever make the first promotional announcement. In your next ministry activity, gauge success by the extent to which you're able to meet the felt needs of those in your congregation.

At the close of your ministry activities, create a place for evaluation. I have a love/hate relationship with evaluations. Many times they're poorly written and only give participants a place to complain. (Again, a sample evaluation is included in the Nuts and Bolts chapter on p. 120.) Instead, create an evaluation that gives you insight into how the activity, event, or Bible study challenged and changed women. How did the Lord speak to her through that Bible study? What was her favorite part of the event? Is there one thing she would change? Above all, gather information, and look for consistency. If a glaring omission or criticism rises to the surface again and again, look more closely at how that portion might be improved. Gather your team to read through evaluations, and let them share their personal responses.

I've realized the best evaluation comes from the women most closely tied to the activity. They have an insider's view of the event's purpose, and they worked the plan. If something didn't work, they're most apt to know how to make improvements for the future.

> What's your response to completing an evaluation? Do you enjoy them? Dread them?

> How have you used them in the past, and how can you improve them in the future?

THE POWER OF KINGDOM PERSPECTIVE IN PROMOTION

Promotion can be creative and fun, but we can never ignore the power of what you're communicating. If your message has eternal ramifications, you must consider the significance of the outcome. Promoting your message or next event is important, but don't forget spiritual transformation in the lives of your women is on the line. Pray that the message of your event or Bible study would be lives transformed by the power of Christ and not the power of your cleverly worded promotion.

THE DANGERS OF SOCIAL MEDIA

When using social media, consider the dangers your women may face as they craft their own messages and absorb others. Here are some pitfalls you may observe in the women you serve.[2]

FOMO This is an acronym for "fear of missing out." While you want your social media messages to give others a feeling that your next event is worth attending, don't create an intentional message that leaves women feeling insignificant.

ISONECTION This word combines the words "isolated" and

"connected" and could be defined as the façade of interaction but not being truly heard, understood or connected with. Isonection[3] speaks to the need people have for true, biblical community.

AFFIRMATION ADDICTION

How many times do the women in your church check to see if they have received likes, comments, or shares? Social media can create a misplaced desire for affirmation when someone checks her Facebook or Instagram account more than ten times a day. Remind women, and yourself, that success in life or on social media isn't measured by the number of likes you receive from your latest post.

APPEARANCE OF PERFECTION

How much time do we spend trying to take the perfect picture or choosing the ideal filter? While you want your social media posts to be of good quality, consider whether your desire is to create an image of perfection or unsustainability. Create posts that show intentionality and authenticity so people can relate. Whether it's admitting your imperfections through the written word or showing a not-so-tidy setting next to the picture perfect image you just created, give women the opportunity to see your struggles.

UNINHIBITED DISCRETION

We don't filter the things we should on social media. This includes immodesty, anger, and unleashing unhealthy emotions. Especially when posting from your ministry account, pause to check your motives. It may even help to have another woman in your ministry review your posts before they go live.

DISTRACTION

Social media is often a distraction—we may use it to avoid something that requires deeper attention. Create boundaries for the amount of time spent on social media, and prioritize focus on the people and tasks in front of you. Give your brain the opportunity to think deeply about a subject. Consider a "no phone" policy in your team meetings to avoid distractions.

BOREDOM

How many times do women use social media as a break? Checking social media can isolate women and may even affect personal interactions.

AVOIDING RESPONSIBILITY

Related to boredom, many women use social media to avoid a more important task at hand. Encourage women to think twice before glancing at their phone when another priority is before them.

CHAPTER 6

EVENTS: WE GATHER TOGETHER

One of my favorite television characters during my high school and college years was a perky cruise director from *The Love Boat*. I would tune in every week and watch Julie coordinate special events on magical cruises that opened doors to the possibility of romance. If I could have chosen one career at that moment in my life, being a cruise director seemed liked the perfect choice. Who doesn't want to dress up, throw parties, and watch love blossom—and all of it in less than sixty minutes?

I fulfilled part of that fantasy when I planned a special event during my early 20s. As a single adult in my church, I helped coordinate a "Love Bus" Valentine's Day progressive dinner for more than fifty single adults in our church. My friend George drove the bus and dressed as the captain while I wore my sailor shoes and navy blazer, living the dream of being cruise director for the evening. I even had people playing "Love Bingo" as we traveled from one location to another. Give me a theme, and I'm game to make the idea a reality—I'll even wear the costume. (Remember those Lucy wigs?)

I can laugh at those thoughts now, but if I were to describe one aspect of women's ministry that I especially love, it's coordinating an event and creating an atmosphere where women want to gather in community and fellowship. Unfortunately, women's events often get a bad reputation. Mother's Day tea parties, elaborate table decor competitions, and fashion shows don't always communicate spiritual growth and disciple-making. Many a blog has been written about the sad state of women's ministry because younger women aren't drawn to cupcakes and cute decorations. Centerpieces, tablecloths, and door prizes can cause women (and many men) to approach women's ministry with the underlying attitude that events don't have substance and are all fluff. Some argue that events take away from the mission of the gospel, instead making the church a social club of elitists who are more concerned with how things look than the hearts of those who come. Yet when the purpose is gospel-centered, and the results are life transformation and biblical community, sign me up. I've never met a cupcake I didn't like.

I have seen events that fit the "fluff" stereotype. I'm sure I've planned a few in my day, but we don't have to perpetuate the stereotype. Events can be more than just a fun gathering of women. They can be a catalyst for friendships, an impetus for mission giving, and a destination where women gather around God's Word and extend the gospel to those who might not come to church on Sunday mornings. Events can be entry points for women who are lost or unengaged. They're connection points for women who need to meet other believers—a place where lives are marked for eternity. They can fuel the fire of discipleship, mission-giving, and worship. Intentional events just take one major ingredient—purpose. As Beth Moore so eloquently put it,

> I still believe in events. Even though I believe the
> priority is doing life as part of a local church. There is
> something about getting away from our day to day
> lives & day to day people & just zoning in for a concentrated
> dose of the things of the Spirit that is really special.[1]

What is your current attitude about events for women? Love 'em or leave 'em? Why?

When was the last time you attended any kind of special event—not just an event within the church?

What drew you to attend?

What made that event special or memorable?

Maybe you haven't considered the biblical purpose or example of events. Throughout Scripture, God's people celebrated with feasts, gathered for the purpose of prayer, and planned celebrations with preparation and invitation. In the Old Testament, the Israelites celebrated seven festivals—reminders of God's provision and faithfulness. These festivals were specific days set aside to honor the Lord—a foreshadowing of the fulfillment found in the Messiah. In the New Testament, Martha prepared meals, the disciples made preparations for the Last Supper, and the early church was characterized in Acts 2 as saying,

> **They devoted themselves to the apostles' teaching, to the fellowship, to the breaking of bread, and to prayer.**
> ACTS 2:42

These events weren't focused on door prizes and centerpieces, but they had the singular purpose of developing biblical community with others in order to point them to Christ. And the biggest event yet to come? Look toward the end of your Bible, and see how Revelation 19 describes the reunion of saints at the wedding feast of the Lamb. I've been to plenty of elaborate weddings, but this is one celebration I don't want to miss. God extends the invitation to anyone who RSVPs to the offer of salvation. I don't know about you, but I don't want anyone to miss that party. You'll find me wearing white.

Have I made my case for the importance of events? If you're still with me on this subject, let's dive into some practical steps for planning your next event. Whether you like it or not, events don't just happen. They take purpose, prayer, planning, personalities, programming, and publicity, and they always come with a price.

EVENTS NEED PURPOSE

Just as your ministry to women needs purpose, events need a reason to exist. The *why* question is the same question you must ask before you plan anything. Ask your team to construct a purpose statement for every event you plan.

Discover ways the event fits into the overall purpose of your local church. Have a vision for the audience you want to reach and the outcomes you'd like to produce. Will your event have a theme? What Scripture will you use to tie everything together? How will you weave these pieces throughout the planning? Are you moving women toward deeper Bible study or missions mobilization? Are you praying for women to place their hope of eternity in Christ as a result of your gathering? As your team meets throughout the planning process, keep the purpose in front of them. Remind them that if it doesn't fit, you must omit.

EVENTS NEED PRAYER

Purpose may be the foundation of your event, but prayer balances that foundational pillar. Before you place a date on a calendar, spend significant time with your team praying for each step. Ask the Lord to reveal the purpose for your event. Is it a need in the community? A need for spiritual development? A desired outcome for unity? Spiritual nourishment or encouragement? Select a woman to serve as your prayer coordinator. Encourage her to enlist others who will pray specifically for the event. Ask her to lead you all in a time of prayer during your planning meetings, and find ways to include her in the actual event. Your prayer coordinator should communicate specific needs to the rest of the team and be willing to think creatively about encouraging others to pray.

How can you give purpose to your next event?

How would this change the way you begin to plan an event for women?

EVENTS NEED PLANNING

You may not consider yourself a detail-oriented person, but events take significant planning. As one of my minister friends once declared, "You all have a lot of vision, but I want to know how you are going to execute that vision." Part of planning your event is setting up processes that will help your event succeed. Here are few questions to consider when planning your next event.

- **WHEN AND WHERE?** Decide on the date and location. Consider the overall church calendar, holidays, and school breaks. Know there is no perfect date without conflicts, but nailing down the date is a vital piece of the puzzle.

- **WHEN DO THINGS NEED TO BE DONE?** Develop a time line of when things need to be accomplished prior to the event. Keep a checklist of when each task is completed.

- **WHAT'S THE SCHEDULE FOR THE EVENT?** Outline the schedule of the event. What time will you open the doors? How much time will you spend in worship? Speaking? Eating? Will you charge for the event or ask for a donation? Will you have tickets that you will need to sell? How and when will they be available?

- **WILL THIS EVENT INCLUDES A SPEAKER?** Will it be someone within your congregation or an outside speaker? Have you considered budget and expenses?

- **WHAT ABOUT FOOD?** Will women in the church prepare the food, or will you pay an outside caterer? How much will it cost? How will you serve the meal? Have you considered preparation and cleanup in the plan?

- **HOW MANY VOLUNTEERS DO YOU NEED?** What responsibilities will they have? Do you have different people for each task?

- **WILL YOUR EVENT INCLUDE DOOR PRIZES OR GIVEAWAYS?** Who will be responsible for this area? When will you give things away during your schedule? How will you give them away?

- **WILL YOU NEED SOMEONE TO RUN THE SOUND OR ANY MEDIA DURING THE EVENT?** Will this include a cost, or will someone donate his or her time?

- **WILL YOU OFFER CHILDCARE?** How much will it cost? Will women need to help cover this cost in the registration?

- **HOW WILL YOU PUBLICIZE THE EVENT?** Do you need someone to design artwork? How will you utilize social media? How will you encourage women to come and bring others?

- **WILL YOU HAVE A MINISTRY PROJECT ATTACHED TO THE EVENT?** Is there someone who can coordinate this aspect? Will it be donations or an offering? How will you deliver those donations?

- **HOW WILL YOU HANDLE REGISTRATION?** How many volunteers do you need in this area? Will you have name tags or a card that gives you information for follow-up?

All of these details and questions may seem a bit overwhelming, but when you begin to put each process in place, your event will run smoothly as you've anticipated each step along the way.

What type of a leader are you? Are you more of a visionary, or do you enjoy having a specific plan to execute? Or are you a mix of both?

If you tend to be one or the other, whom can you invite to help you in your weakness?

EVENTS NEED DIFFERENT PERSONALITIES

The Event Team

We've already discussed the importance of leadership teams for successful ministry. Your events also need a team of dedicated servant leaders who are passionate about executing an event. Your leadership team should consist of a variety of women in different ages and stages of life, and your event team should be diverse as well. If you're in a smaller church, your leadership team may be the same as your event team, but consider how many women you can include, and find women to serve in the areas where they're gifted. Divide responsibilities amongst as many women as possible. When you do, these women will "buy in" to the event, invite others, and become natural cheerleaders.

Depending on the kind of event you're planning, consider including these various team members:

COORDINATOR	This will most likely be you—the women's ministry director. This person builds the team, divides the tasks, and brings cohesive vision to the event. The coordinator provides leadership and direction, along with an environment for collaboration and creativity.
PRAYER LEADER	As discussed earlier, this woman enlists a team of women to pray for the event and leads prayer times for the planning team. She will also coordinate any prayer elements at the actual event.
REGISTRATION/ FINANCE COORDINATOR	(This role may be divided between two people, if necessary.) This woman handles the receiving and spending of money. She monitors the ticket sales, recruits volunteers to help with registration at the event, and works with the church staff to make sure everything is in place. This person may also recruit greeters—the front line when women walk in the door. She may consider whether you can provide sponsorships to women who can't afford the registration cost.

FOOD COORDINATOR	This person coordinates the kind of food you'll serve and how you'll serve it. She can also ensure that it adheres to any health code restrictions or policies your church may have in place. Encourage her to take a variety of diets and allergies into consideration for each event.
WORSHIP AND AUDIO/VISUAL COORDINATOR	People often overlook the sound team—until they realize their necessity. Secure someone ahead of time, provide details of what you'll need, and thank that person profusely.
CHILDCARE COORDINATOR	There's likely already a person at your church who handles childcare. Ask that person for input regarding recruitment of workers, the cost of childcare, and the need for childcare. Don't forget: single moms many times avoid events because they have no one they can trust to watch their children.
DECORATOR	Find someone who enjoys and has the talent for making things beautiful. While this might seem like one of those fluff details, consider how many women watch popular home remodeling shows or follow decorators on Instagram. When women walk into your event and they observe a beautiful and creative environment, it tells attendees you have thought about and planned for them. Find women who are resourceful in this area—those who know how to repurpose and use items already available.
MINISTRY PROJECT COORDINATOR	Will you include a particular ministry focus during the event? Is there an upcoming mission trip that has a request? Is there a pregnancy center that needs donations? Can you adopt an unreached people group and plan a prayer strategy during the event? Help women understand that events aren't just about "them" but about seeing and serving your community and the world outside the church walls.
GIVEAWAYS AND DOOR PRIZES COORDINATOR	Believe it or not, some women love asking local businesses for door prizes or finding the perfect giveaway at an event. While this isn't a necessity, it often creates a fun atmosphere. Don't make this the focus of an event but a "bonus" surprise. Create powerful and memorable moments where gifts or door prizes promote excitement and anticipation.

HOSPITALITY LEAD	If you're hosting an out-of-town speaker or special guest, enlist someone to be by that person's side from beginning to end. If you're coordinating the event, don't assume you'll have extra time to spend with the speaker. You will likely be busy making sure everyone executes the details, so hand this responsibility off to another woman who will make sure your special guest is well cared for.

SECURING A SPEAKER

In addition to the various personalities involved in an event team, you must consider whether you'll secure the personality of an outside speaker for the event. Many years ago, churches often looked for women who felt called in this area and would enlist them for special events. While this still happens, times have changed. Today churches may not have the budget to bring in outside speakers, and many times guest speakers aren't as effective as a local might be because they don't know the audience. Instead, consider asking someone within your congregation to provide inspiration or Bible study. Choose someone with godly wisdom, and give her a clear idea of what you'd like for her to communicate. Aim for faith over funny. Remember, your main purpose is to draw women closer to Christ—not just to serve up a night of entertainment.

If you choose to enlist an outside speaker, or even if you use someone within your church congregation, here are some suggestions as to how to ensure a good experience for both parties.

PROVIDE DETAILS UP FRONT.	Early on, communicate your purpose, the schedule, how long she has to speak, the anticipated audience, and even what the dress might be for the event.
PAY HER EXPENSES.	Does she have a set honorarium? Will you pay her mileage or extra expenses? Consider not only her speaking time but the time it takes for her travel and preparation.
PRAY FOR HER.	Pray for your speaker, and send cards throughout your planning process to let her know you are praying for her preparation.

PICK SOMEONE TO HOST THEM.	Designate one woman to stay by your speaker's side and accommodate any specific requests. In addition, consider whether you'd like to give your speaker additional gifts. Take into account how she's traveled and whether your gift will be easy to transport. Flowers, big baskets, and breakables aren't airplane friendly—if that's how your speaker is traveling.

EVENTS HAVE A PRICE

I still remember attending a planning meeting for a women's team that wanted to offer a weekend retreat. They had great ideas and were excited to offer this event at the price of $50. As I listened to what the retreat entailed, I quickly wrote a list of the expenses they would most likely incur. After thirty minutes, I gently asked, "How many women do you expect to attend?" Their goal was fifty women. I did the math—not always my greatest strength. They had a total of $2,500 in anticipated revenue and weren't sure if the church had budget money to contribute. I added up the cost of a speaker, food, retreat center, publicity, and so forth. I showed them my tally—the final cost was $75 per person. My intention wasn't to crush their dreams but to help this team understand the price of events. They quickly re-evaluated and made adjustments.

If you want to coordinate a successful event and garner the blessing of your church leaders, learn how to be a responsible steward and count the cost. Be realistic about expenses, including last-minute or unexpected add-ons that may rear their ugly heads as the event gets closer. Find someone on your team who can manage the budget and keep everyone on track. Financial responsibility exemplifies a ministry to women that is trustworthy.

EVENTS NEED GOOD PUBLICITY

Don't minimize the importance of publicity when planning your next event. If you have the budget or you have a talented graphic artist in your congregation, start with good design. If you want your event to stand out, spend the time, money, and effort to use attractive art that appeals to younger women.

Look for creative ways to spread the news about your event, and make sure to take advantage of social media. Ask your team to share the information on their personal social media platforms to create common interest.

EVENTS REQUIRE EVALUATION AND CELEBRATION

Post-event letdown is a real thing. You've cleaned up the mess, packed the car, and may be ready for a nap. Do those things, but don't forget one important last step—evaluation and celebration.

Plan a post-event meeting with your team fairly soon after the event is over. If you wait more than two weeks, it's likely you'll forget a few things and your team may be ready to move on. Instead, create a final meeting with your team to celebrate what God did through the event. Write thank-you notes, carve out time for fellowship, and allow women time to share stories of life change. If you had response cards or evaluations at the event, brag on the ways God spoke to the hearts of those who attended and celebrate the hard work that went into the planning process.

Remember to give the team that planned the event an opportunity to provide feedback. Without being a party pooper, find ways to express constructive criticism. One of my

ICEBREAKERS: LOVE 'EM OR LEAVE 'EM

There are plenty of women who deplore forced interaction—especially if they've walked into your event alone. Even the words "play a game" can send introverts into the corners. Nevertheless, consider how icebreakers may move women out of their seats and create opportunities for discussion. Don't force women into your next icebreaker, but don't exclude icebreakers; they are a way to engage in conversation. Use them wisely. A good icebreaker will enhance the purpose of your event and not simply add an activity. If you're looking for specific ideas, use the Internet to find a plethora of inspiration.

close friends provided our team with this idea—stars and wishes. Our team first spent time making a list of "stars"—the things that went well. We celebrated those victories and thanked God for His favor. Second, we spent time discussing "wishes"—those things we wished had gone differently. We didn't place blame on people, and we didn't find ways to be super critical. We spent this time discussing how things could be different next time in addition to things we learned in the process. Above all, if you want team members to return, focus on the positives and minimize criticism.

CREATIVE EVENT IDEAS

It's possible you have a mental image of what a women's event might entail, but here are some creative ideas that might challenge the way you view events. Instead of doing the same thing every year, mix things up and try something new! Here are a few suggestions.

SIMULCASTS

If you're looking for a way to gather women around God's Word and feature a well-known Bible teacher, consider hosting a simulcast. LifeWay offers these events several times a year. Churches from around the world gather women together for the purpose of Bible study and prayer. Many of them offset the cost of a simulcast by charging for individual tickets, but they also invite others in their community to join together. Simulcasts are a fun and easy way to coordinate an event.

CRITICAL ISSUES

Women are passionate about social justice issues such as human trafficking, refugee care, orphan care, domestic violence, and abortion. Create a symposium on one or more issues. Bring in experts to discuss how your women can make a difference and provide experiential, learning activities. Give women tools and resources that will equip them to make a difference.

SPIRITUAL DISCIPLINES

Focus an event on explaining various disciplines such as prayer, Bible study, solitude, and fasting. Create a prayer experience during the event, or extend this event from a few hours to an entire weekend retreat. Provide journals for women to express how the Lord has spoken to them during the event.

FUNDRAISING EVENTS FOR MISSIONS OR MINISTRY PROJECTS

Coordinate a fundraising event surrounding an upcoming ministry project—it's a great way to raise awareness regarding the place you're going or people you're serving. It allows the community to jump in too. For example, one of my best friends leads an event at my former church called "The Gift Goes On." Women spend an evening fellowshiping and shopping from local vendors to raise funds for a foster care and adoption ministry within the church. On top of that, the event features a silent auction. The annual event typically raises more than $50,000 in one evening.

ATHLETIC EVENTS

Sponsor a 5K race and donate the money raised from the entry fee for a ministry project. This will not only create an exciting event for women, but it will also raise awareness throughout the community—outsiders will flock to participate.

EVENTS FOR A SPECIFIC AUDIENCE

Consider special events for widows, moms of young children, or business entrepreneurs. Find women in your congregation who have a passion for the targeted group, and encourage them to use their passion as a way to minister to others.

LEADERSHIP DEVELOPMENT EVENTS

Attend a local leadership event with your ministry team. If you want to raise up new leadership, find conferences that will equip and excite new leaders for innovative and fresh aspects of ministry.

OUT-OF-TOWN EVENTS

Women love a good getaway. Consider taking a group to a retreat or arena event. These events often take travel coordination, but they give the leader a chance to enjoy an event without planning all of the details.

How could you incorporate a creative event that would attract a different audience?

How could you adapt one of these ideas for your church?

FINAL THOUGHTS ON EVENTS FOR WOMEN

- **INCORPORATE BALANCE.** As you plan events, consider how you might include the following elements: prayer, worship, discipleship, missions, evangelism, and building community. You don't necessarily have to create separate events for each of these—just find ways to make sure your event features each of them.

- **CREATE A DESTINATION FOR FELLOWSHIP AND FRIENDLY ATMOSPHERE.** At one event, I decided to introduce myself to another woman who was sitting alone. I quickly discovered she was a visitor and had come hoping to meet new people. We carried on a conversation throughout the event while others who attended never gave her a second thought. They missed a big opportunity to encourage this woman who was looking for friendship. Don't forget the saying, "People aren't looking for a friendly church. They are looking for friends."

- **PLAN FOR LAST-MINUTE CANCELLATIONS AND NO-SHOWS.** Unfortunately, people will bail at the last minute. Anticipate it, plan for it, and pray for others to take their place. Life happens, so don't be surprised when the Evil One wants to throw up roadblocks at the last minute.

- **WHEN WOMEN STOP COMING TO YOUR EVENT.** Often, I hear the moans of leaders who say, "Women just aren't coming to our events." This isn't a new problem. Luke 14 describes a parable of a big banquet. The banquet was planned and prepared. They had sent out invitations. The response? Luke 14 says,

> But without exception they all began to make excuses.
> The first one said to him, "I have bought a field, and I must
> go out and see it. I ask you to excuse me." Another said,
> "I have bought five yoke of oxen, and I'm going to try
> them out. I ask you to excuse me." And another said,
> "I just got married, and therefore I'm unable to come."
>
> LUKE 14:18-20

If you see attendance for your events tapering off, you may want to take the opportunity to consider the way your events are structured, whether you're meeting the needs of your women (spiritual, emotional, physical), and how your events fit into the larger mission of your church. What small changes could you make? Are there large structural adjustments to be made? Do you need to gather a small group of women to help you evaluate the effectiveness of events? Choose women who come to your events—and some who don't—for a variety of perspectives.

- **WHEN YOUR EVENT NEEDS TO DIE.** Let's face it. If you've been doing an event every year for several years, and your attendance is slowly dying, it's time to evaluate its effectiveness. Consider whether its purpose is still viable. Consider whether it's still relevant. Don't forget to utilize event evaluations (p. 125) and be open to implement the feedback that you receive consistently. Seasons come and go, so don't plan an event because it's what you've always done. Sometimes it's best to let it go away—even for a time.

Maybe you don't see yourself as Julie, the cruise director, who loves planning events. But you just might be the catalyst or the one holding the life preserver for another woman who needs Jesus. Go ahead and plan that event. Let the One who rescues do the work you can't.

MESSY MINISTRY:

THE MINISTRY OF

PAIN AND CRISIS

———

A woman was walking down a busy street and fell into a large hole. Hoping someone would come and quickly pull her out of the hole, she began yelling for help. A doctor passed by but didn't come to her aid. A pastor walked by, saw her in the hole, and promised to pray for her. Desperate and alone, the woman nearly gave up hope when a close friend jumped in the hole and landed beside her. Seeing her friend, she said, "Why did you jump in the hole with me? Now we're both down here without anyone to save us!" The friend gently looked at her despondent friend and said, "You're right. But I've fallen in this hole before, and I know the way out."

This might be an old illustration, but it's a poignant picture of how women approach ministering to other women in crisis. We can choose to ignore the crisis in front of us, promise to pray for them without really helping, or jump in with both feet and walk beside the one who is hurting. We either under-stand others' pain because we've been there before, or we're willing to walk beside them step-by-step, showing them God's faithfulness and freedom.

I've personally played all three roles in this scenario. It's easy to be the doctor—the one who knows the answers but simply refuses to see the need right in front of her. I could see "T" standing outside my church office, but I was "busy" typing details for an upcoming Bible study. She quietly got my attention anyway and said, "Hi. Could you pray for my hands?" Startled to find someone at my door, I invited her in and asked about her hands. She began to share about a new job she had taken at a local box company. The work was hard, and the manual labor of working with cardboard had left her hands chapped and bloody. As a single mother, she quietly sobbed that she needed the job to take care of her two little boys. We sat there, praying God would sustain her, provide for her, and heal her hands. That day and that particular moment were markers for my ministry—a firm reminder to never put projects before people. Be mindful of the women standing at your door, and be available. Since that day, I've continued to watch T raise her boys, and I've seen God's faithfulness in her life—and His kindness to heal her hands.

While this isn't an exhaustive list, here are common areas where women in crisis may seek your help:
- Prodigal children
- Depression and/ or suicide
- Anxiety
- Trauma
- Eating disorders
- Abortion
- Infertility
- Death
- Addiction
- Domestic abuse
- Marital issues
- Divorce
- Adoption and foster care
- Finances
- Incarceration
- Natural disasters
- Refugees
- Cancer or other sickness
- Unforgiveness

I've also been "the pastor" in the story—the one who had spiritual answers, but abandoned the hurting. "M" was a cheerleader during our high school days. She continued cheering at a prestigious university and later had a successful career in broadcasting. From the outside, she appeared to have everything, until one evening when her decision to drive under the influence caused a fiery crash, killing an elderly couple. Having access to our county jail, I visited her. Unlike most people, chaplains many times have the ability to sit knee-to-knee with those they've come to meet. I hadn't seen her in years and wasn't sure if she'd remember me since I was the quiet yearbook editor—not part of the popular crowd like she was. We connected, and I shared my concern. I asked her about her relationship with the Lord, promised to pray for her, and spent time doing that very thing. Unfortunately, that was about as far as I went. One visit. One letter. Years of incarceration followed. I kept one of her letters in my desk as a reminder to pray for her and especially for her mom who attended my church. While I did pray, I regret that prayer was about as far as my involvement went. I was the minister who promised to pray, yet I continued to walk by, unwilling to stay with her in the hole until she got out. Thankfully, she is now out of prison and has a desire to use her story to point others to Christ.

And then there is "S." She and her husband were fairly new to our church and sat behind my husband and me in the balcony. As we casually got to know them, we discovered he was a former student pastor at a nearby church. We didn't ask a lot of questions about why they weren't still in vocational ministry, assuming the husband's job at a non-profit organization took him a different direction. After church one Sunday, S asked if I had time to meet for coffee. I'm always up for a coffee conversation, so we set a date. When she arrived, I realized she wasn't drinking coffee. Instead, the purpose of our meeting was for her to share her story. I listened for more than two hours—hearing about her struggle with anorexia and cutting, the time she'd spent with doctors, involvement with in-house and facility care, and even how it cost them her husband's ministry position. Mostly, I sat in silence, weeping and wanting to understand her struggles, her past, and her pain. What began as a coffee date developed into a friendship that continues today. Our daughters are friends, and our husbands go kayaking together. I can honestly say I haven't always jumped in the hole with my friend, but she did life with me when I faced a crisis. She was one of the first to check on me during my most difficult circumstances, brought me food, and showed up on my doorstep just to spend time praying with me. She exemplified this verse from 2 Corinthians,

> **And our hope for you is firm, because we know that as you share in the sufferings, so you will also share in the comfort.**
>
> 2 CORINTHIANS 1:7

Because she had suffered, she was by my side, providing both spiritual comfort and meeting my physical needs to help me climb out of a hole of despair.

There are many biblical stories of compassion and ministering to those in crisis. Consider the story found in Mark 2 of four friends who literally tore through a roof to get their paralytic buddy to Jesus. These four men knew Jesus could heal their friend physically, but they were graciously surprised when he left with his sins forgiven.

In his book *Everybody's Normal Till You Get to Know Them* John Ortberg describes this Mark 2 story as "the fellowship of the mat."[1] These roof-crashers did everything they could to get their friend to Jesus. As Ortberg says,

> **It is a very vulnerable thing to have someone carry your mat. When somebody's carrying your mat, they see you in your weakness. They might hurt you if they drop you.**[2]

When women minister to other women in crisis, they carry each other's mats.

But don't forget—each of us has our own mats, our own burdens. Ortberg reminds us,

> Let the mat stand as a picture of human brokenness
> and imperfection. It is what is "not normal" about me.
> It is the little "as-is" tag that I most desire to hide. But it is
> only when we allow others to see our mat, when we give and
> receive help with each other, that healing becomes possible.[3]

STAGES OF GRIEF AND LOSS

- Shock
- Expression of emotions
- Depression and loneliness
- Physical symptoms of distress
- Panic
- Sense of guilt
- Anger and resentment
- Resist turning to pre-loss state
- Realization of hope
- Affirm reality

Ministering to women in pain may mean doing everything you can to bring them face-to-face with Jesus. You may have to go after that friend. You might have to break down barriers. But you may also see healing that brings glory to the Father.

Jesus, too, did a fair amount of ministering to women in crisis. He valued them, spoke to them, healed them, and forgave them. Whether it was a bleeding woman, a shamed woman at the well, or a woman caught in adultery, Jesus provided the specific help each woman needed for her situation. He listened, He cared, and He cured. How can we do the same today? How can we follow in His footsteps?

If you're honest, which of the three are you most like—the doctor, pastor, or friend? Why?

In your own life, who helps carry your mat?

Is it hard for you to let others serve you and see your weaknesses?
Why or why not?

How can you personally care for those in crisis?

How can you, as a leader, help others to be friends to those in crisis (and
avoid being like the pastor and doctor in the story)?

THE THEOLOGY OF SUFFERING

It's difficult to minister to women in crisis unless you approach the topic with a
theological understanding of suffering. Most women struggle with the question
of why God allows suffering. It can also be the linchpin question, the one that
determines whether a woman will trust God in the midst of her pain. I don't have
room to be exhaustive on this topic, but I do think we should look at some basic
concepts before diving into the practical ways you can minister to women in crisis.

Suffering Began in the Garden

You don't have to read beyond Genesis 3 to see where suffering and brokenness
began. The garden of Eden was a real, physical location filled with order and har-
mony. Adam and Eve enjoyed perfect communion with God. When sin entered

TIPS ON VISITING SOMEONE IN THE HOSPITAL

- Keep it short—less than ten minutes.
- Pray with them.
- Don't promise things you won't do.
- Avoid being a comedian.
- Don't over-share information about similar situations.
- Don't sit on hospital beds.
- If a family member wants to visit longer, step outside the room for longer conversations.

the garden, our world became marked with suffering, death, and decay. As theologian Don Carson once explained,

> What Jesus seems to presuppose is that all the sufferings of the world—whether caused by malice [as in Luke 13:1-3] or by accident [as in Luke 13:4-5]—are not peculiar examples of judgment falling on the distinctively evil, but rather examples of the bare, stark fact that we are all under sentence of death.[4]

Christ and His Suffering

Jesus met women in the midst of their sorrows, but He was also a man of sorrow and suffering. Jesus wept with Mary and Martha at the tomb of Lazarus, and He completed His own suffering on the cross. Christianity is unique among religions and offers comfort because our Savior experienced suffering. Isaiah vividly described this suffering:

> He was despised and rejected by men, a man of suffering who knew what sickness was. He was like someone people turned away from; he was despised, and we didn't value him. Yet he himself bore our sicknesses, and he carried our pains; but we in turn regarded him stricken, struck down by God, and afflicted. But he was pierced because of our rebellion, crushed because of our iniquities; punishment for our peace was on him, and we are healed by his wounds.

ISAIAH 53:3-5

Our Present Sufferings and Future Hope

Being one with Christ also means that we, too, will suffer. Jesus told His disciples that they would drink the cup that He drank and be baptized with the same baptism. Jesus told them not to be surprised if they encountered persecution. Paul begged the Lord to remove his "thorn in the flesh" in 2 Corinthians 12:7, yet the outcome wasn't God removing Paul's suffering but Paul learning to find sufficiency in God's providence and grace.

God can use suffering as part of your spiritual journey. As you minister to those who are suffering, recognize we may not always know or understand the ways of God, but we can know Him and His attributes. Innocent people will suffer. Babies will die. Good people will endure hardship. We can't escape the suffering of our broken world, but we can rest in the character of God's goodness and His perfect plan, which includes an end to suffering when everything will be made right. We can rest in the promise of Romans 8:

STEPS TO BEING EFFECTIVE WHEN YOU MEET WITH A WOMAN IN CRISIS

- Pray (for yourself, for her, and for the situation).
- Listen to her story.
- Listen for her feelings and validate them.
- Encourage her with Scripture.
- Create healthy boundaries and steps of action.
- Reach out to others when you're not equipped.
- Pray again.

> For I consider that the sufferings of this present time are not worth comparing with the glory that is going to be revealed to us.
>
> ROMANS 8:18

PRACTICALLY SPEAKING

So what are the essentials of ministering to women in crisis? Where do you start? How can you begin to see women as Jesus sees them? Let's consider some practical steps you can incorporate in your ministry to women and specifically to women in crisis.

The Practice of Presence and Confidentiality

Whether you have much experience in ministering to women in crisis or not, there's one way you can make a difference—show up. While the world may run away from crisis, the church should be a place to lean in. I lived most of my life in Oklahoma, a place where tornadoes wreak havoc. I'm always amazed how within minutes of a disaster volunteers mobilize. Within hours, feeding units deploy, and chaplains begin the painful process of ministering to those left in the wake of destruction. I've watched them pray, but mostly I've watched them listen. They are present with the hurting—hearing their stories and letting the wounded express their grief. I've also witnessed the power of touch—knowing when it's appropriate to hug, hold a hand,

SCRIPTURE APPROPRIATE FOR VARIOUS CRISES

- Abortion: Psalm 139:13
- Anxiety: 1 Peter 5:7
- Anger: Proverbs 29:11
- Death: 1 Corinthians 15:55
- Depression: Psalm 62:5
- Finances: Matthew 6:25
- Forgiveness: Ephesians 4:32
- Loneliness: James 4:8
- Self-esteem: 2 Corinthians 3:18
- Sickness: Psalm 6:2
- Tiredness: Isaiah 40:29

or put a hand on a shoulder in a way that says, "I'm here, and I care."

You may not be called to respond to a natural disaster, but it's likely people will share their life stories with you—lives that may have been tossed and turned by the storms of death, addiction, or abuse. Use the ears God has given you to listen. Listening is your most valuable tool in crisis ministry.

With listening comes the responsibility of confidentiality. Unless someone is in a dangerous or abusive situation where you have a legal obligation to inform authorities, consider how to respond with appropriate boundaries. Far too often women have used hurtful information as gossip in the disguise of prayer requests.

The Ministry of God's Word and the Local Church

Besides the practice of presence, don't neglect the power of sharing God's Word when ministering to hurting women. If you're like me, when crisis hits, you run to God's Word. It can encourage you and empathize with your hurts. Many of the psalms are written as a lament, expressing the fears and grief of the writer. As one of my counselor friends, Kaye Hurta, explains,

> Lament provides us with physical language for entrusting
> God with our sorrow. It helps us process our sorrow honestly,
> and it invites hope to enter in. Lament also provides a structure
> for expressing our sorrow to God. It is a great way to notice
> and name our sorrow by holding our complaint to God AND
> our trust in the truth of His character simultaneously.[5]

Keep a list of various topics or crises you may encounter along with specific Bible verses you can use for encouragement. You may not have the right words to say, but God's Word does. One of my ministry mentors kept a stack of bookmarks she had made with Scriptures appropriate during crisis. She kept them available for women who found their way to her office and confided in her. She listened well, and always pointed them directly to the Bible.

A few years ago, I led a women's Bible study on Wednesday evenings at my church. As a long-time member, I had a pretty good handle on knowing most of the women there. But I soon realized there were many unfamiliar faces in the crowd, and I began wondering how out-of-touch I had become. Who were these women, and where had they come from? Over the next few weeks, I began to hear their stories, and I quickly discovered many of them started coming to our church through an addiction recovery program. While many of them weren't ready to attend worship on Sunday mornings, they discovered their next step was getting involved in one of our women's Bible studies. I was reminded of how God's Word gives life and brings healing to those who have been in dark places. Open your studies to a variety of women, and welcome those who are hurting.

HOW TO MEET THE PHYSICAL NEEDS OF THE HURTING
- Ride share
- Conversation
- Books or helpful resources
- Freezer meals
- Childcare
- Housework/yard work
- Gift cards

When people die or relationships break, times of crisis may become times when the local church can step in to meet practical needs and offer the hope of the gospel. The ministry of meeting tangible needs may be the first step to beginning a spiritual conversation. I might have once scoffed at the thought of a casserole being part of a ministry to women, but meeting a physical need may open many doors for the gospel. Whether it's food, clothing, or shelter, your hospitality serves as a bridge to break down barriers and walls.

The Importance of Professionals and Referrals

Most ministry leaders are not professional counselors. I don't even score high in mercy when I take a spiritual gift assessment! Nevertheless, I'm not excused from showing mercy and compassion to those who need it. At the same time, you and I must also know our limitations. All of us are called to be ministers of reconciliation, but not all of us are professionally qualified to offer clinical counseling. Know professionals, and maintain a list of referrals at your fingertips.

Where do you begin? Look at your church congregation. Do you have licensed counselors within your church? Look in your community. Have you developed relationships with Christian counselors? Do you know the names of shelters? Crisis pregnancy centers? Are you familiar with organizations that offer help? Do you know the difference between biblical counselors, licensed counselors, and psychiatrists who have medical degrees and the credentials to prescribe medication? Learn these things, and develop a network of mental health professionals whom you can use as resources when necessary.

Above all, the church cannot be silent on issues involving abuse or mental illness. If a woman in an abusive situation comes to you, call the authorities, and get her out of the abusive situation and into a safe place. She may be hesitant, but you have an obligation to help remove her from harm.

For many women in your ministry, the words of Psalm 88:18b, "Darkness is my only friend" ring all too true. More than ever, women are seeking help for their specific situations. We must recognize women's brokenness and make it part of the conversation. No one escapes suffering or pain, but we're called to invite women to follow Jesus and be reconciled to Him. As my pastor Daryl Crouch recently wrote,

> Jesus reconciles people to God, but he will not restore
> all that sin has stolen until he returns again. So until then,
> we serve people in their suffering. We voluntarily walk
> with them through the maze of their emotional, physical,
> relational, and spiritual challenges. Rather than viewing
> them as new recruits to serve our church goals, we
> eagerly join God's redeeming work in their lives.[6]

Certainly there's no one-size-fits-all when it comes to ministering to women in crisis. But you can be wise and intentional about the way you equip your women's ministry team and the women in your church to listen, counsel, and resource well those around them who may be struggling. Your leadership and example in this matter is extremely important. What a blessing to be a part of God's ministry of reconciliation in bearing up the brokenhearted and pointing them back to Him in their most vulnerable times.

What resources to aid women in crisis does your church already have in place?

What areas of your church's crisis ministry could your women's ministry team help strengthen? Take this opportunity to see where God might be prompting you to use the gifts represented on your team. (This is not meant to be a time for complaint or criticism of church leadership.)

Take a moment to prayerfully consider your approach to women in crisis. Ask God to show you:

• Areas in which you might need more firm, yet appropriate, boundaries.

• Areas in which you need to be more tender-hearted.

Journal a prayer to God regarding women you know who are currently in crisis. Ask Him to give you discernment, wisdom, strength, and a clear vision as to how your ministry to women in crisis can best honor Him.

CHAPTER 8

OUTREACH AND EVANGELISM: MINISTRY TO OTHERS

——

My friend Lorna was in town, and I was excited she had time for lunch. She always challenges me to think about my community and how I'm reaching others. This lunch was no different. Before we could order pizza, she blurted out, "Don't let me forget to talk about *Sesame Street.*" Wait. *What? What does Sesame Street have to do with our lunch?* As we sat down, I took the bait. "OK, tell me about *Sesame Street.*" She excitedly explained a bit of history about the public television show that has enraptured millions of children since 1969. Lorna shared how the creators of the show wanted to showcase a real neighborhood of diversity. They wanted to emulate something that already existed but failed to find it. They looked across the United States, and no matter where they explored, they couldn't find an accurate representation of blended cultures, economic status, and community. Instead, they decided to create a street that projected a "future" neighborhood—one they would create and use to slowly change societal attitudes about acceptance and friendship. They even threw in a big yellow bird, a grouchy creature who lived in a garbage can (Who wouldn't be a grouch if they lived in a garbage can?), and catchy theme song lyrics.

Lorna got excited about viewing our Christian culture and ministry to women through this lens. Lorna questioned me, "What if we projected a future of biblical community? What if we started creating an atmosphere of seeing our communities as heaven will look—every tribe and every nation?" As I processed what she was saying, these words resounded in my heart and mind: *We often tell women to pray, to give, to send, and to go. I think we need to add another word. What if we added the word, "Welcome"?*

> My salvation was a result of a librarian who had the courage to go in a county jail. County jails and prisons need women who will serve as chaplains.
> —Barbara

Those words continue to burn within me as I consider the importance of outreach and evangelism in ministry to women. We are pretty good at being disciple-makers. We are pretty good at praying for others and ministering to those in need. Yet, too many women in our community don't feel welcome in our ministry. As one of my friends said years ago, "Our church is really good at buying coats for those who need them. We're lousy at putting the coats on the people who need them." Does this describe your current ministry to women?

What might a practical welcome look like for you personally?

As a ministry leader?

In your ministry?

In what area of outreach are you most effective?

Where do you need to make improvements?

On a scale of 1 to 10, with 10 being the most effective, where would you rank your current ministry with regard to outreach?

Least Effective							Most Effective		
1	2	3	4	5	6	7	8	9	10

Will you take the challenge to see beyond yourself and go after others? Consider how your ministry to women can put out the welcome mat and open the door for those who need a relationship with Christ and the community. Let's start creating a culture and community that reflect the bigger body of the worldwide capital "C" Church and begin to see ministry to women as more than a country club for women who all look alike.

A BIBLICAL PERSPECTIVE

If you've been a student of God's Word for a while, you're probably familiar with the story of Philip and the Ethiopian eunuch in Acts 8. But how much attention have you given to the verses prior to that story?

> So those who were scattered went on their way preaching the word. Philip went down to a city in Samaria and proclaimed the Messiah to them. The crowds were all paying attention to what Philip said, as they listened and saw the signs he was performing. For unclean spirits, crying out with a loud voice, came out of many who were possessed, and many who were paralyzed and lame were healed. So there was great joy in that city.
>
> ACTS 8:4-8

Here we find Philip leaving Jerusalem after the stoning of Stephen. He ended up in a city in Samaria. Don't forget that Samaritans were hated by Jews, yet Acts 1:8 gives the command to go not only to "Jerusalem, [to] all Judea and Samaria, and to the end of the earth." I've often heard Samaria compared to the larger region outside of Judea, but rarely do I hear people describe Samaria as going to the places where we aren't accepted—or more accurately, where we don't accept others. Yet Philip preached the Word and proclaimed the Messiah. Miracles happened, and there was great joy in the city. We don't know what Philip's past thoughts were of Samaria, but he seemed to have taken Jeremiah's words to heart:

> Pursue the well-being of the city I have deported you to. Pray to the LORD on its behalf, for when it thrives, you will thrive.
>
> JEREMIAH 29:7

Philip's obedience to take the gospel to a new city with no believers, or people like himself, should encourage us to be faithful to take God's Word into whatever community He places us.

Jesus, too, had a lot to say about our mission. His final words in Matthew 28 are the challenge to "Go ... and make disciples of all nations" (v. 19). He left us with a global challenge, but He also reminded us of the individual challenge in Luke 15:

> I tell you, in the same way, there will be more joy
> in heaven over one sinner who repents than over
> ninety-nine righteous people who don't need repentance.
>
> LUKE 15:7

Jesus always found time to speak to the individual, to his or her heart, and to his or her need for forgiveness. How can we not do the same in our ministry to women within the local church?

KNOWING HOW TO SHARE YOUR FAITH

Label a teaching session on "evangelism" and see how many women show up. It's likely they will use the excuse, "I don't know how to share my faith." They might share their fears in regard to sharing their faith—fear of rejection, fear of difficult questions, and fear of unknown responses. Fear is generally driven by the unknown or what we can't control. The reality is the word *evangelism* often deters women instead of causing them to embrace the call to share with eager attentiveness.

If you desire to have balance in your ministry to women, you need to teach women practical ways to feel confident in sharing the gospel. Your ministry should be outwardly-focused—that echoing of God's heart for the world that we discussed earlier in the book. You need to help new believers feel confident in their newfound faith and help them learn how to take the next steps in discipleship. Intentional discipleship results in good evangelism, and good evangelism should result in ongoing discipleship. Both go hand-in-hand—not one without the other. Disciple-makers who believe in multiplying and replicating disciples should strive for women to come to faith. So where do you start?

Evangelism methods have shifted and changed over the past forty years. If you lived through the days of Evangelism Explosion or the Four Spiritual Laws, you'll remember simple tracts and directed questions that were extremely effective in their day but have lost momentum in recent years. With a culture that has rejected moral absolutes and embraced religious skepticism, it has become ever more difficult to use the same methods. Please don't misunderstand me. Those methods can still be effective. I'm not against personal evangelism or tracts. Instead, we must help women understand the process of evangelism—how to begin gospel conversations and how to see people as people and not as projects that must be fixed. As David and Norman Geisler defined *evangelism* in their book *Conversational Evangelism,*

> **Evangelism is every day and in every way helping your nonbelieving friends to take one step closer to Jesus Christ.[1]**

How can you practically equip your women for this kind of evangelism? First, help them determine people in their lives who need the gospel. Challenge them to make a list and share it with others. Whether it's a neighbor, a family member, or someone in the community, awareness of lostness should be the first step.

Second, encourage women to pray—really pray. Whether women in your ministry meet for Bible study or for fellowship, encourage them to share their lists and to actively begin praying for gospel conversations. Pray more than once—make it an ongoing point of prayer. How differently would your prayer time look if you stopped praying for sick people and starting praying for those who are spiritually sick?

Third, help women be aware of daily, divine appointments. Remember Philip? He was sharing the gospel in Samaria and found himself on the road to Gaza. He was sensitive to the angel's prompting and was in the right place at the right time when the Ethiopian had questions. Help women see their daily routines as divine appointments. Help them always be ready to share Christ with those they encounter. Remind women that people die, relationships break, and suffering is all around us. When those situations arise with neighbors, coworkers, and family, these circumstances are times to lean in and offer the hope only Christ can give.

Fourth, create spaces in your ministry where evangelism is talked about and emphasized. Encourage your Bible study groups to invite women with spiritual

> **We have a group for moms and close to fifty of those who attend self-identify that they are not connected with a church. We provide food, a speaker, childcare, and a creative activity for women to develop friendships and community with other moms in our community.**
> **—Sarah**

questions. Make it a point in every Bible study to extend a salvation invitation, and don't assume everyone in your group has had a true conversion experience. Leave an open chair in small groups as a reminder of the woman who needs to fill that spot. Provide events that draw non-believers, and then offer invitations for them to respond. Offer experiences—such as mission trips—that give women a focused time to share their faith.

Finally, help women make the most of every conversation that might help a non-believer take one step closer to Jesus. Equip your women with an easy way to share their own salvation stories and also to share the simple steps of following Christ.

How are you currently encouraging women to share their faith?

In what ways can you practically equip them to be more confident in the area of evangelism?

How can you incorporate the overall outreach plans of your church into your ministry to women?

These steps all begin with equipping women to have confidence in knowing how to share their faith. The two simplest ways I know to share your faith are through listening and telling your personal story.

1) Sharing Your Faith Through Listening

Listening is one of the most neglected areas of leadership development, yet James reminded us,

> **Everyone should be quick to listen,**
> **slow to speak, and slow to anger.**
> JAMES 1:19

As we truly learn the art of listening, we begin to hear the stories of others and build trust in relationships. As Selma Wilson once said on her blog,

> As leaders, it's tempting to get so caught up in our own voice, in what we have to say, we drown out everyone else. The truth is that your voice is only as strong as your ability to listen.[2]

Listening says, "I want to know you, and I care about you" instead of, "I want you to conform to my belief system."

As you begin to listen to others and truly hear their stories, look for opportunities to ask good questions. Uncover the reasons they haven't followed Christ, and begin to build a bridge to the gospel. David and Norman Geisler use this acronym for LISTEN in their book *Conversational Evangelism*:

> We need to LISTEN carefully to what our nonbelieving friends say so we will know how best to talk to them. As we listen to them we also want to *learn* their story by *investing* some time in them. As we're doing this, we also want to *search* for gaps in their beliefs. As we talk to them we also want to *throw* some light on the conversation by clarifying their beliefs. Yet we also want to *expose* the cracks in their beliefs and surface uncertainty by asking them thought-provoking questions. Finally we want to *navigate* the conversation carefully by keeping the three *D*s in mind (Doubt, Defensiveness, Desire).[3]

What part of listening is most difficult for you?

What three concrete steps might you take to become a better listener?

Listening is only the first step in sharing the gospel. The second is empowering women to know how to share their personal salvation stories.

2) Sharing Your Faith By Telling Your Personal Story.

Look for opportunities to equip women in your ministry to write their stories, to shorten them to a minute, and to practice sharing them with others. Encourage women to include a description of what their lives were like before they met Christ, their personal encounters with Christ, and the difference Christ has made in their lives.

While listening to and helping women craft their personal testimonies are important, you need to give women a simple way of presenting God's Word to an unbeliever.[4] Of course, there are many simple ways to present the gospel, so find one that helps your women feel comfortable and competent in sharing their faith.

> In your ministry, who shares her story well? How could that person help you train women to feel more comfortable sharing their own stories?

WHO IS IN YOUR NEIGHBORHOOD?

Do the women in your church all look alike? How can you see the needs in your community? Opportunities for evangelism begin where you see the hurts within your community. Whether it's a local school that needs volunteers to tutor children or a nearby crisis pregnancy center that needs helpers or donations, find practical ways to make a difference in your community. Check the demographics in your area and ask if your church is a good representation of that demographic. Are there internationals in your community, and how are you seeking to include them or minister to them?

> How would you answer the question, "If our church didn't exist, would the community notice?"

All of these questions point to the importance of community involvement and outreach. Many times ministry to women in the local church can become inwardly focused and not outwardly motivated. So how do you begin to help women in your church see the needs in your community?

How can you engage with the hurting and marginalized?

START WITH PRAYER-WALKING.

If you're not familiar with prayerwalking, there are many resources that will help you understand prayerwalking, or "praying on-site with insight"—a definition I often use and found in the book *Prayerwalking*.[5] Designate a day for groups of women to pray over different areas in the community. Teach women how to walk in their neighborhoods and pray for families. Gather women in vans and encourage them to observe areas of need in your community, such as schools, city officials, first responders, areas of poverty, healthcare facilities, and assisted living centers. The list is numerous, but it's a way to intentionally observe your community with a fresh perspective and burden for those who need Christ.

How can you encourage women in your church to prayerwalk on their own or with someone else?

DISCOVER WAYS WOMEN IN YOUR CHURCH ARE ALREADY INVOLVED IN THE COMMUNITY.

Most likely there are already women involved and passionate about your community. Whether they volunteer at a local senior center or help at a women's shelter, seek out those who are already connected and find ways for other women to join them.

Create a list of things your women are currently doing in the community. Ask: How can we partner together and shed light on what is already happening?

PRAYERWALKING HOW-TOS

1. Plan a prayerwalk and give women instructions and a map.
2. Pray as a group or as an individual.
3. Pray Scripture out loud.
4. Pray as you're prompted by things you see as you walk.
5. Pray for opportunities to have conversations with others.
6. Debrief with your group after your prayerwalk.

CONNECT WITH COMMUNITY LEADERS.	Do you know your local leaders? Reach out to them and ask about the needs they see on a daily basis. Be a champion of those who are intimately involved in the day-to-day workings within your community and offer them your support. Invite them to be present at one of your events and recognize them for their contribution.
ENCOURAGE EVERY ASPECT OF YOUR MINISTRY TO CONNECT WITH AN OUTREACH OPPORTUNITY.	Maybe you have several small groups. Ask each leader to think of one way their group can engage with an outreach opportunity. Plan an event that connects with a community need. For instance, plan a back-to-school activity and encourage women to bring school supplies. Direct them to write prayer cards to teachers at a nearby school, or possibly plan a teacher appreciation breakfast. Not only will you include women in your church, but you'll include others outside your church who want to be involved. The ideas are endless!

BEYOND YOUR NEIGHBORHOOD: GLOBAL MISSIONS

History is filled with godly women who have had a heart for the nations. If you're not familiar with the names Elisabeth Elliot, Amy Carmichael, Martha Myers, Lottie Moon, or Ann Judson, spend time getting to know these heroes of the faith who lived their lives following the Lord through sacrifice and passion to take the gospel to the ends of the earth.

Better yet, get to know some women who are still doing this, and find ways to expand your women's ministry to have a global perspective. There are many women today serving in countries where people are hostile to the gospel, yet they are fulfilling their calling to follow Christ no matter what the circumstance or location.

How do you connect women to global missions? What are some ways you can involve women in your local church to reach the nations and echo God's heart for the world?

Here are some simple ideas to get you started.

- **ADOPT AN UNREACHED PEOPLE GROUP.** Depending on whose statistics you read, there are thousands of people groups who have never heard the gospel. Find an unreached people group by looking at websites such as joshuaproject.net or imb.org. Begin praying for the people, learn about them, and keep their names in front of the women in your ministry. Be creative in the ways you remind women to pray for open doors and for receptivity to the message of eternal life.

- **BE INVOLVED WITH PEOPLE FROM OTHER COUNTRIES IN YOUR OWN COMMUNITY, INCLUDING NEARBY UNIVERSITIES.** It's heartbreaking to learn of the number of international students who come to the United States for education who are not invited into an American home. It's estimated that more than 1 million international students attend a U.S. university every year. I was reminded of this a few years ago when our son brought home two students from Korea. I was confused when one of them asked to see our backyard. Our yard wasn't expansive or unusual, so I thought his request was interesting. After showing him around, he told me that it was the first time a family had invited him into their home. What he said next was the best: "I grew up watching American sitcoms and had a picture of what a backyard was. Yours was exactly what I had in mind!"

- IF YOU LIVE IN A RURAL AREA WITH A LOCAL UNIVERSITY, DON'T THINK THAT YOU DON'T HAVE INTERNATIONAL STUDENTS. I learned a couple of years ago that several Nepalese students attended a small two-year school in northwest Oklahoma. Our state collegiate ministry provided them with their first Bibles and sought ways to connect them to Christ. Another women's ministry at a nearby church provided linens and toiletries for students when they discovered many of them arrived with only one suitcase in their possession.

> We're looking into local organizations that rescue women from the sex trade and prostitution and discovering ways we can partner with them.
> —Kimberly

> We try to incorporate outreach and evangelism into what our church is already doing, whether that's a back-to-school event where we distribute backpacks with free school supplies or help with a community Easter egg hunt. I always plan to hand out small gifts to women at events that attract children because lots of children equal lots of women.
> —Amy

- **ORGANIZE A GROUP AND ATTEND A LOCAL INTERNATIONAL FESTIVAL.** Visit an international grocery store or connect a women's event to a different culture. Invite an international group to attend one of your events, and ask them to share ways your group can begin to build a bridge of acceptance and inclusion. If you don't have access to something like this, consider bringing the cultural experience to your next women's event. For example, show women how to share their faith using henna. Set up stations where women can create henna artwork on their hands as a way to create gospel conversations.

- **SUPPORT MISSIONARIES CONNECTED TO YOUR LOCAL CHURCH.** Your church may be closely connected to a specific family serving overseas. Seek ways your ministry to women can support them through prayer, projects, and practical needs. Send care packages to families, but always ask first about their specific needs. A friend of mine grew up in South America. Well-meaning people sent boxes of feminine hygiene products since there were two girls in the family. What they didn't know was those products were readily available in the city where they lived. She often joked about the abundance of supplies they had stacked in their storage that took years to consume.

- **ENCOURAGE WOMEN TO PURCHASE FAIR TRADE PRODUCTS, OR PROVIDE WAYS FOR WOMEN TO BUY THEM AT ONE OF YOUR EVENTS.** Several organizations sell fair trade products that provide incomes for women who are living in developing countries or provide an avenue to make money and avoid becoming a victim of human trafficking. LifeWay Christian Resources partners with many such organizations, so make sure to check out those opportunities in LifeWay retail locations. One of my favorite organizations is WorldCrafts, a division of Woman's Missionary Union. You can check out a variety of products available at worldcrafts.org.

- **ORGANIZE AN INTERNATIONAL MISSION TRIP FOR WOMEN.** This is a huge undertaking, but the long-term benefits outweigh the organization it takes for international travel. When women see the needs of others firsthand, when they put boots on the ground in a developing country, or when they're given opportunities to share their faith in the midst of language and cultural barriers, not only are lives influenced in the country you visit, but the hearts of your women are forever changed and engaged with those they meet. Taking women to another country will increase their faith and expand their worldviews. It will make the Great Commission come alive and fuel their desires to engage with others who don't look like them, act like them, or have the same belief system.

One way I will connect women to global missions:

TIPS FOR PLANNING AN INTERNATIONAL MISSION TRIP

1. Pray about where to go.

2. Learn about where you're going and connect with the work being done.

3. Select women who are physically, spiritually, and emotionally ready for travel.

> We started a compassion dinner for women and highlighted different ministries, such as a local pregnancy center. The last one focused on world hunger. Women thought they were getting a catered meal, but ended up with beans and rice! We followed it up with sharing three different ministries in developing countries. We used it as a fund-raiser for these ministries and it was a success!
> —Jacki

4. Ensure everyone has obtained a passport and has appropriate immunizations and documents for the country of travel. Some countries require an additional visa, so allow plenty of time to obtain all travel documents.

5. Meet as a group several times prior to the trip to answer questions, prepare spiritually, and be informed of logistics and the work you'll do once there. Learn how you'll share the gospel appropriately and equip your team to be ready to share their personal salvation stories.

6. Remind women that A mission trip is not a vacation or photo opportunity. The goal is to find appropriate ways to share the gospel. If you're working with missionaries who are already on the field, remind your team that they're joining others in their work. The trip will not be according to your own agendas. The local partners don't have time or capacity to be tour guides. And, speaking of photos, be culturally appropriate in regard to sharing your experience online—especially if you're working in a sensitive area—to protect the people whom you're serving and the partners you're serving alongside.

7. Raise financial support and prayer support from others. Connect the entire church to pray and support the team so everyone in your ministry has invested in the trip. Ask your pastor for a commissioning time during one of your services so the entire congregation is praying.

8. Pack appropriately. Have a good understanding of what attire is acceptable. Ask missionaries if you can bring them items they miss or need for their work. Consider whether you'll be carrying your suitcase for long distances. You may want to opt to take everything in a carry-on bag instead of a large suitcase.

9. Eat a flexi-cookie. In other words, your best travel companion on a mission trip is flexibility and adaptability. Your expectations or plans may not be what you or your team experience, but extend grace in those moments and acclimate to the situations you face.

10. Find ways to minister to the missionaries while you're there. They may be experiencing loneliness or discouragement with their work. Be an encourager, provide prayer support, and love them while you're there. It may be the greatest reward of your trip.

11. When you return, share your experience with others in your local church. Be mindful that your group will be more excited because they had the experience, but it's always appropriate to share what God did on the trip.

Outreach and evangelism should be one of your most important goals as you develop a ministry to women in your local church. Without them, the women in your local church may easily become inwardly focused and develop an entitlement mentality. Let's build neighborhoods of diversity and acceptance. When we do, our ministries just might look a little more like heaven.

How does your church intentionally practice missions?
□ Domestic:

□ International:

Name one thing you enjoy about missions.

Name one thing about missions that challenges you.

On a scale of 1 to 10, with 1 being not engaged or enthusiastic and 10 being very engaged and enthusiastic, where does your church congregation fall regarding missions?

Not Engaged and Enthusiastic   Very Engaged and Enthusiastic
1   2   3   4   5   6   7   8   9   10

The women in your ministry?

Not Engaged and Enthusiastic   Very Engaged and Enthusiastic
1   2   3   4   5   6   7   8   9   10

Name two ways you can implement missions in your women's ministry events and discipleship.

CHAPTER 9

NUTS AND BOLTS: PRACTICAL TOOLS TO HELP IN YOUR DAY-TO-DAY MINISTRY

We've come to the end of the larger content of this resource, but I'm the first one to consider all the subjects you won't find in the previous chapters. That's why we've added the following pages of practical how-tos and lists. Even so, always remember your local ministry to women is unique. Your context and culture are unique. Adapt these resources and use them as guidelines, not standards. They are tools you can and should adapt as you see fit.

MINISTRY SURVEY

Whether you're beginning a new ministry to women in your local church or rebuilding an existing ministry, assessing the needs of women begins with offering a survey. Consider the main questions you want to ask, and determine the process of gathering information. Some churches choose to ask women to complete a written survey made available through Bible study groups, church services, or other church distribution channels. Some women choose to offer an online survey and advertise it through normal church channels and social media avenues. The main thing is to keep it brief, maintain focus, and determine the purpose for gathering information. Design questions with simple answers that avoid open-ended questions when possible. (They're more difficult to process and more time-consuming.) Consider whether the survey should be anonymous or if you're looking for specific names of potential volunteers. Offer an incentive or a prize for those who complete the survey as a way to garner more responses.

The following survey is designed for women already attending your church—not unchurched women in your community. You may consider editing these questions to create a shorter version.

SAMPLE SURVEY

Please complete the following to help our church plan ministry to and with women.

What's your age group?
__ 18-29 years old
__ 30-39 years old
__ 40-49 years old
__ 50-59 years old
__ 60-69 years old
__ More than 70 years old

Which describes you best?
__ Single, never married
__ Single, divorced
__ Single, widowed
__ Married, no children
__ Married with small children
__ Married with teens
__ Married with adult children

Which describes you best?
__ Working full-time
__ Working part-time
__ Homemaker
__ Retired

Which time of the week works best for your schedule when planning women's activities?
__ Daytime during the week
__ Evenings during the week
__ Weekends

Which time of the year works best for your schedule to attend a Bible study?
___ Winter
___ Spring
___ Summer
___ Fall

Of the following, which interests you the most in women's ministry?
__ Prayer ministry
__ Outreach ministry
__ Bible studies
__ Discipleship groups
__ Mission projects
__ Events

What kind of fellowship/events interest you?
__ Women's retreats
__ One-time women's events
__ Luncheons
__ Home fellowships/coffees
__ Other: _____

When is the best time for you to attend a Bible study? (*check all that apply*)
___ Weekday morning
___ Weekday lunch time
___ Weekday evening
___ Sunday evening
___ Online Bible study

How many weeks can you commit to a Bible study? (*check all that apply*)
___ Four weeks
___ Six weeks
___ Ten weeks
___ Other (*please specify*):

What kind of Bible study most interests you? (*check all that apply*)

___ Bible study that includes video teaching

___ Bible study without video teaching

___ Bible study with personal study during the week

___ Bible study with no personal study during the week

___ Bible study focused on a specific topic

___ Bible study focused on a book of the Bible

___ Recovery support groups

___ Book study

___ Other (*please explain*):

Name a study you would be interested in doing.

I would participate in the following:

__ Evangelism training

__ Prayer ministry

__ Short-term mission trips

    __ United States

    __ International

__ Community mission projects

Other ideas?

The following community ministries interest me:

__ Literacy

__ Tutoring

__ Pregnancy center

__ Hospital ministry

__ International ministry

__ Nursing home ministry

__ Recovery ministry

__ Food pantry/clothing closet

__ Other:

__ I am already involved with this community ministry (*please explain*):

I would be willing to help with the following at a women's event:

__ Publicity

__ Food preparation and organization

__ Decorations

__ Hospitality

__ Registration

__ Door Prizes

__ Childcare

__ Prayer

__ Ministry project

I currently attend (*check all that apply*):

__ Sunday School

__ Worship

__ Women's Bible study

__ Women's events

What's your greatest need right now?

__ Spiritual encouragement and prayer

__ Bible study

__ Fellowship with other believers

__ Mentoring

__ Connection to community ministries

Other (*please explain*):

Have you been previously active in our church's ministry to women?

__ Yes

__ No

If not, why?

Describe one thing you would like implemented in our ministry to women:

What's the best way to communicate with you? (*check all that apply*)

__ Worship guide

__ Sunday morning announcements

__ Mailings

__ Facebook

__ Twitter

__ Instagram

__ Email

__ Information table in foyer

__ Text message

EVALUATIONS

You may have a love/hate relationship with evaluations like I do. They often are a source of frustration when women complain about issues out of your control or when they seem to pick on something that's a personal preference. Even so, evaluations provide feedback that can be valuable and help you tell the stories of life change. Just like a survey, keep evaluations brief and focus on what the Lord has done in the heart of the person—not whether they liked the food. Again, consider whether you want personal information or if you want the evaluation to be anonymous. When women provide their names and contact information, you have the ability to follow-up with decisions they've made or to address a concern that's bothersome.

In addition to asking attendees for feedback, remember that the team who helped organize the event you're evaluating will have the most insight. Most likely, they'll already know what went right and how things can be improved in the future.

SAMPLE EVALUATION

Name:

Email:

Phone:

How did you learn about this event? (*check all that apply*)
__ Church website
__ Church announcement
__ Friend
__ Women's e-newsletter
__ Women's Bible study
__ Facebook
__ Twitter
__ Instagram
__ Women's information booth in church foyer
__ Other (*please specify*):

This event/Bible study:
__ Exceeded my expectations
__ Met my expectations
__ Did not meet my expectations

The best thing about this event/Bible study:

If I could change one thing, it would be:

The way God spoke to me:

Other comments:

MEETING AGENDA

If you're a ministry leader and you're planning team meetings, always include an agenda. It'll help your team stay on point, keep you on time, and add value for your time together. Once again, the sample provided should be adapted to fit your time frame, objectives, and what you want to accomplish within the meeting time.

SAMPLE AGENDA

Leadership Team Monthly Meeting

DATE
PRAYER AND DEVOTION
PURPOSE
REPORTS

MINISTRY PROJECTS
• Current projects
• Future projects
• Areas of concern or needs

DISCIPLESHIP
• Upcoming Bible studies
• Evaluating current studies
• Potential leaders
• Future plans

COMMUNICATION
• Promotion of events and ongoing activities
• Creative ideas for promotion

EVENTS
• Upcoming event details
• Progress with specific team
• Areas of concern

BUDGET
• Overall budget
• Specific concerns or praises

NEW BUSINESS
CLOSING PRAYER

SAMPLE TEAM COVENANT

Team covenants are a great tool to use with current and new members of your team. They set the expectations between the leader and the team members while offering accountability that can be measured. While you should always design a covenant that works specifically for your team, the following is a sample you can use when thinking through items to include.

I Agree to Adhere to the Following Commitments ...

Cooperate with the established church leadership and support the plans and activities of the church (Heb. 13:17).

Be faithful in attending the weekly worship service along with the other highlighted services throughout the year (Heb. 10:25).

Believe and teach that the Bible is the divine, inspired Word of God, and that Scriptures are "truth, without any mixture of error"[1] (see 2 Tim. 3:16).

Attend the servant team meetings, contribute ideas, and seek to maintain unity within the team. I will honor the call God has placed on each of our lives. I agree to uphold and affirm one another as servants of our Lord Jesus Christ and seek to edify and respect one another on a continuing basis (Rom. 12:10).

I will commit to be a faithful steward with those whom God has entrusted to me by ministering to members and reaching out to guests (1 Pet. 5:2-4).

I will commit to grow in my personal walk with Christ and develop my spiritual gifts, taking advantage of resources that will sharpen me as a team member. I agree to invest in one another by sharing resources, experiences, ideas, and current information about our respective activities and needs. This will enable us to identify practical ways to assist one another (Luke 9:16; 2 Tim. 1:6).

Whether married or single, I commit to be an example "in speech, in conduct, in love, in faith, and in purity" (1 Tim. 4:12).

I will commit to be "above reproach," recognizing some things are lawful but are not expedient for my witness for Christ as a leader (1 Tim. 3:2-3; 1 Cor. 6:12).

I will give joyfully and sacrificially to the Lord by contributing to the church with my tithes and offerings (Mal. 3:10; 2 Cor. 9:6-8).

I will endeavor to make verbal and lifestyle witnessing a part of my life. As I remain true to my individual calling, I agree to partner in pursuing a great calling—a calling to kingdom. I will create space in my life to allow for participation in kingdom-building activities. I commit to impacting the lostness "to the end of the earth" for the glory of God (Acts 1:8; Col. 4:5-6).

Signature:
Date:

SPIRITUAL GIFT SURVEY

Self-awareness through a variety of assessments is not only helpful for your ministry teams, but these assessments provide opportunities for you to connect the right women to the right place of ministry. If you're just forming a ministry team, encourage women to complete various assessments as they discover their own leadership potential and ways to work together for optimal performance. In addition to the sample Spiritual Gifts Survey (see p. 131), here are some helpful resources.

(see p. 131)

- □ PLACE Ministries (available at www.placeministries.org)
- □ *5 Voices: How to Communicate Effectively with Everyone You Lead*, by Jeremie Kubicek and Steve Cockram (available at 5voices.com)
- □ *StrengthsFinder 2.0*, by Tom Rath (book includes individual code for assessment)
- □ *Leading from Your Strengths: Building Close-Knit Ministry Teams*, by Eric Tooker, John Trent, and Rodney Cox (B&H Publishing Group)

INCLUDING MINISTRY WIVES

No two ministry wives are alike, yet there are common needs among many of them who struggle with prayer support and friendship. As a women's leader, consider how you can include ministry wives in the activities you organize, but don't be offended if their level of participation is less than you might desire. Seek to develop healthy relationships with ministry wives and consider the following ways you can include them.

1. PRAY FOR YOUR MINISTRY WIVES. Often, they'll be guarded and wary to share personal struggles and family situations. Don't be offended. Instead be their biggest prayer champion. Extend your friendship and respect their personal boundaries.

2. SOME MINISTRY WIVES ARE THE LEADERS OF YOUR MINISTRY TO WOMEN. Some ministry wives are the cheerleaders for your ministry to women.

Some will prioritize their church involvement in other areas such as student ministry, children's ministry, or through general support to their husbands. Whatever your situation, accept them for who they are.

3. WHEN APPROPRIATE, AND IF THEY'RE INCLINED, INCLUDE MINISTRY WIVES ON YOUR TEAM OR WITHIN YOUR ACTIVITIES FOR WOMEN. If they enjoy public speaking, encourage them to be a speaker at one of your events. If they enjoy leading a small group, encourage them in that capacity. Just as you seek out the spiritual gifts and passions of other women, learn the passions and talents of your ministry wives.

4. CONSIDER PRACTICAL WAYS YOU CAN SHOW GRATITUDE FOR YOUR MINISTRY WIVES. Shower them with gifts, provide free childcare when appropriate, or treat them with a date night.

5. DON'T USE YOUR MINISTRY WIVES AS A WAY TO GET INFORMATION TO THEIR HUSBANDS. Don't assume ministry wives have all the information. Just because these women have an inside connection with their husbands, don't hand them a list of things you want them to address over the dinner table. In addition, don't assume they know everything that's happening at church. Like most marriages, there's a lot more to talk about than the daily rundown of church activities.

WORKING WITH MALE STAFF MEMBERS

Whether you're leading a ministry to women as a paid staff member or as a non-paid servant leader, you'll most likely be working with a majority of male staff. The phrase, "Men are waffles and women are spaghetti," can often be played out in ministry. While men tend to compartmentalize, women have a bigger tendency to mix everything together. A good leader understands how to navigate these differences and work toward healthy communication and practices. The following are some considerations:

- ARRANGE MEETINGS IN A PROFESSIONAL SPACE, SUCH AS AN OFFICE WITH WINDOWS, AND HAVE AN OPEN DOOR POLICY. Always meet during regular office hours and when others are present.

- IN THE SAME WAY, CONSIDER HOW YOU TEXT A MALE STAFF MEMBER. Keep it simple and to the point. Evaluate how text messages (and even emails) can be received. Ask yourself, *If his wife saw my text message, would it come across appropriately?*

- MEET FACE-TO-FACE WHEN NEEDED INSTEAD OF PRESENTING A PROBLEM OR ISSUE OVER EMAIL. Emails are void of emotions and are not always received in the way you sent them. If there are problems, address them face-to-face.

- **COMMUNICATE HOW MUCH TIME YOU NEED.** Stick to that time frame, and provide an agenda prior to the meeting.

- **MINIMIZE SMALL TALK AND BE DIRECT.** Don't interrupt, and use concise statements to make your point.

- **AVOID BEING OVERLY EMOTIONAL OR RESPONDING WITH A VICTIM MENTALITY.** Remain professional at all ministry meetings. In other words, "toughen up." Selma Wilson once wrote,

> Being a leader means debating ideas, hearing objections, arguing (sometimes passionately arguing) for the best in an opportunity to advance or a problem to solve. Don't take it personally when your ideas get shot down. The goal is not that *you* win but that the organization or team you lead wins.[2]

- **IF YOU'RE COMING WITH A PROBLEM, THEN OFFER POSSIBLE SOLUTIONS.** If you don't have a solution, be upfront about asking for their advice. Present the issue or problem in a positive way and don't attack others personally.

- **CONSIDER HOW THEY THINK, RATHER THAN HOW THEY FEEL.** While it may come naturally to discuss your ministry and the women in your church by how you feel, be intentional to communicate concretely and logically.

- **BE DIRECT WITH YOUR REQUEST AND DON'T BE AFRAID TO NEGOTIATE.** Understand how to interpret their "no" responses.

- **BE RESPECTFUL OF THEIR AUTHORITY AND POSITIONS.** Acknowledge the impact their leadership has in your church and in your ministry. Work to partner joyfully with them in ministry.

- **INVITE THEM TO BE INCLUDED IN YOUR NEXT MINISTRY ACTIVITY.** Encourage them to welcome women, offer a prayer, or be an observer. More importantly, commit to pray for them.

SPIRITUAL GIFTS SURVEY

DIRECTIONS

This is not a test, so there are no wrong answers. The Spiritual Gifts Survey[3] consists of eighty statements. Some items reflect concrete actions; other items are descriptive traits; and still others are statements of belief.

• Select the one response you feel best characterizes yourself and place that number in the blank provided. Record your answer in the blank beside each item.
• Do not spend too much time on any one item. Remember, it is not a test. Usually your immediate response is best.
• Please give an answer for each item. Do not skip any items.
• Do not ask others how they are answering or how they think you should answer.
• Work at your own pace.

Your response choices are:

5—Highly characteristic of me/definitely true for me
4—Most of the time this would describe me/be true for me
3—Frequently characteristic of me/true for me—about 50 percent of the time
2—Occasionally characteristic of me/true for me—about 25 percent of the time
1—Not at all characteristic of me/definitely untrue for me

_____ 1. I have the ability to organize ideas, resources, time, and people effectively.
_____ 2. I am willing to study and prepare for the task of teaching.
_____ 3. I am able to relate the truths of God to specific situations.
_____ 4. I have a God-given ability to help others grow in their faith.
_____ 5. I possess a special ability to communicate the truth of salvation.
_____ 6. I have the ability to make critical decisions when necessary.
_____ 7. I am sensitive to the hurts of people.

_____ 8. I experience joy in meeting needs through sharing possessions.
_____ 9. I enjoy studying.
_____ 10. I have delivered God's message of warning and judgment.
_____ 11. I am able to sense the true motivation of persons and movements.
_____ 12. I have a special ability to trust God in difficult situations.
_____ 13. I have a strong desire to contribute to the establishment of new churches.
_____ 14. I take action to meet physical and practical needs rather than merely talking about or planning to help.

15. I enjoy entertaining guests in my home.
16. I can adapt my guidance to fit the maturity of those working with me.
17. I can delegate and assign meaningful work.
18. I have an ability and desire to teach.
19. I am usually able to analyze a situation correctly.
20. I have a natural tendency to encourage others.
21. I am willing to take the initiative in helping other Christians grow in their faith.
22. I have an acute awareness of the emotions of other people, such as loneliness, pain, fear, and anger.
23. I am a cheerful giver.
24. I spend time digging into facts.
25. I feel that I have a message from God to deliver to others.
26. I can recognize when a person is genuine/honest.
27. I am a person of vision (a clear mental portrait of a preferable future given by God). I am able to communicate vision in such a way that others commit to making the vision a reality.
28. I am willing to yield to God's will rather than question and waver.
29. I would like to be more active in getting the gospel to people in other lands.
30. It makes me happy to do things for people in need.
31. I am successful in getting a group to do its work joyfully.
32. I am able to make strangers feel at ease.

33. I have the ability to plan learning approaches.
34. I can identify those who need encouragement.
35. I have trained Christians to be more obedient disciples of Christ.
36. I am willing to do whatever it takes to see others come to Christ.
37. I want to help people who are hurting.
38. I am a generous giver.
39. I am able to discover new truths.
40. I have spiritual insights from Scripture concerning issues and people that compel me to speak out.
41. I can sense when a person is acting in accord with God's will.
42. I can trust in God even when things look dark.
43. I can determine where God wants a group to go and help it get there.
44. I have a strong desire to take the gospel to places where it has never been heard.
45. I enjoy reaching out to new people in my church and community.
46. I am sensitive to the needs of people.
47. I have been able to make effective and efficient plans for accomplishing the goals of a group.
48. I often am consulted when fellow Christians are struggling to make difficult decisions.
49. I think about how I can comfort and encourage others in my congregation.
50. I am able to give spiritual direction to others.

_____ 51. I am able to present the gospel to lost persons in such a way that they accept the Lord and His salvation.

_____ 52. I possess an unusual capacity to understand the feelings of those in distress.

_____ 53. I have a strong sense of stewardship based on the recognition that God owns all things.

_____ 54. I have delivered to other persons messages that have come directly from God.

_____ 55. I can sense when a person is acting under God's leadership.

_____ 56. I try to be in God's will continually and be available for His use.

_____ 57. I feel that I should take the gospel to people who have different beliefs from me.

_____ 58. I have an acute awareness of the physical needs of others.

_____ 59. I am skilled in setting forth positive and precise steps of action.

_____ 60. I like to meet visitors at church and make them feel welcome.

_____ 61. I explain Scripture in such a way that others understand it.

_____ 62. I can usually see spiritual solutions to problems.

_____ 63. I welcome opportunities to help people who need comfort, consolation, encouragement, and counseling.

_____ 64. I feel at ease in sharing Christ with nonbelievers.

_____ 65. I can influence others to perform to their highest God-given potential.

_____ 66. I recognize the signs of stress and distress in others.

_____ 67. I desire to give generously and unpretentiously to worthwhile projects and ministries.

_____ 68. I can organize facts into meaningful relationships.

_____ 69. God gives me messages to deliver to His people.

_____ 70. I am able to sense whether people are being honest when they tell of their religious experiences.

_____ 71. I enjoy presenting the gospel to persons of other cultures and backgrounds.

_____ 72. I enjoy doing little things that help people.

_____ 73. I can give a clear, uncomplicated presentation.

_____ 74. I have been able to apply biblical truth to the specific needs of my church.

_____ 75. God has used me to encourage others to live Christlike lives.

_____ 76. I have sensed the need to help other people become more effective in their ministries.

_____ 77. I like to talk about Jesus to those who do not know Him.

_____ 78. I have the ability to make strangers feel comfortable in my home.

_____ 79. I have a wide range of study resources and know how to secure information.

_____ 80. I feel assured that a situation will change for the glory of God even when the situation seems impossible.

SCORING YOUR SURVEY

Follow these directions to figure your score for each spiritual gift.

1. Place in each box your numerical response (1-5) to the item number which is indicated below the box.

2. For each gift, add the numbers in the boxes and put the total in the TOTAL box.

LEADERSHIP	+	+	+	+	=	
	Item 6	Item 16	Item 27	Item 43	Item 65	TOTAL
ADMINISTRATION	+	+	+	+	=	
	Item 1	Item 17	Item 31	Item 47	Item 59	TOTAL
TEACHING	+	+	+	+	=	
	Item 2	Item 18	Item 33	Item 61	Item 73	TOTAL
KNOWLEDGE	+	+	+	+	=	
	Item 9	Item 24	Item 39	Item 68	Item 79	TOTAL
WISDOM	+	+	+	+	=	
	Item 3	Item 19	Item 48	Item 62	Item 74	TOTAL
PROPHECY	+	+	+	+	=	
	Item 10	Item 25	Item 40	Item 54	Item 69	TOTAL
DISCERNMENT	+	+	+	+	=	
	Item 11	Item 26	Item 41	Item 55	Item 70	TOTAL
EXHORTATION	+	+	+	+	=	
	Item 20	Item 34	Item 49	Item 63	Item 75	TOTAL
SHEPHERDING	+	+	+	+	=	
	Item 4	Item 21	Item 35	Item 50	Item 76	TOTAL
FAITH	+	+	+	+	=	
	Item 12	Item 28	Item 42	Item 56	Item 80	TOTAL
EVANGELISM	+	+	+	+	=	
	Item 5	Item 36	Item 51	Item 64	Item 77	TOTAL
APOSTLESHIP	+	+	+	+	=	
	Item 13	Item 29	Item 44	Item 57	Item 71	TOTAL
SERVICE/HELPS	+	+	+	+	=	
	Item 14	Item 30	Item 46	Item 58	Item 72	TOTAL
MERCY	+	+	+	+	=	
	Item 7	Item 22	Item 37	Item 52	Item 66	TOTAL
GIVING	+	+	+	+	=	
	Item 8	Item 23	Item 38	Item 53	Item 67	TOTAL
HOSPITALITY	+	+	+	+	=	
	Item 15	Item 32	Item 45	Item 60	Item 78	TOTAL

GRAPHING YOUR PROFILE

1. For each gift place a mark across the bar at the point that corresponds to your TOTAL for that gift.

2. For each gift shade the bar below the mark that you have drawn.

3. The resultant graph gives a picture of your gifts. Gifts for which the bars are tall are the ones in which you appear to be the strongest. Gifts for which the bars are very short are the ones in which you appear not to be strong.

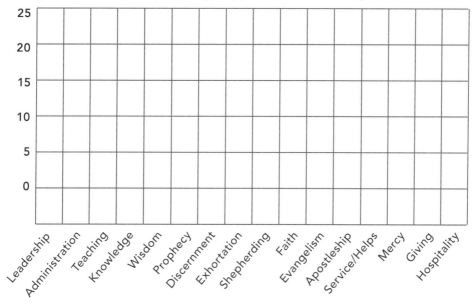

Now that you have completed the survey, thoughtfully answer the following questions.

The gifts I have begun to discover in my life are:

1. _____

2. _____

3. _____

• After prayer and worship, I am beginning to sense that God wants me to use my spiritual gifts to serve Christ's body by _____.

• I am not sure yet how God wants me to use my gifts to serve others. But I am committed to prayer and worship, seeking wisdom and opportunities to use the gifts I have received from God.

Ask God to help you know how He has gifted you for service and how you can begin to use this gift in ministry to others.

ENDNOTES

INTRODUCTION

1. "'Nones' on the Rise," Pew Research Center, published October 9, 2012, www.pewforum.org/2012/10/09/nones-on-the-rise.

2. Tamar Lewin, "At Colleges, Women Are Leaving Men in the Dust," July 9, 2006, www.nytimes.com/2006/07/09/education/09college.html.

3. "Essential," *Merriam-Webster's Dictionary,* June 28, 2018, www.merriam-webster.com.

CHAPTER 1

1. Simon Sinek, "How great leaders inspire action," TEDxPuget Sound, September 2009, www.ted.com/talks/simon_sinek_how_great_leaders_inspire_action.

2. Todd Adkins and Eric Geiger, "5LQ Episode 226: More Lies Leaders Believe with Carey Nieuwhof," 5 Leadership Questions Podcast, February 1, 2018, www.lifeway.com/leadership/?s=carey+nieuwhof.

3. Jonathan Swift, *The Works of Jonathan Swift,* Volume 13 (London), 231.

4. Drew Dudley, "Everyday leadership," TEDxToronto, September 2010, www.ted.com/talks/drew_dudley_everyday_leadership.

CHAPTER 2

1. Tony Merida, *Christ-Centered Exposition Commentary: Exalting Jesus in Exodus* (Nashville, TN: B&H Publishing Group, 2014), 114.

2. Reggie Joiner, as quoted on the blog of Carey Nieuwhof, "Great Ideas," accessed July 19, 2018, https://careynieuwhof.com/great-ideas.

3. Wayne Cordeiro, "Developing a Strong Ministry Team," *Ministry Today,* May 1, 2002, https://ministrytodaymag.com.

4. Peter Drucker, as quoted in Andrew Cave, "Culture Eats Strategy For Breakfast. So What's For Lunch?" *Forbes,* November 9, 2017, www.forbes.com.

CHAPTER 3

1. Robby Gallaty, *Growing Up: How to Be a Disciple Who Makes Disciples* (Nashville: TN: B&H Publishing Group, 2013), 12.

CHAPTER 4

1. Susan Hunt, *Spiritual Mothering* (Wheaton, IL: Crossway Books, 1993), 49.

2. Ibid, 177.

3. Esther Burroughs, *A Garden Path to Mentoring* (Birmingham, AL: New Hope Publishing, 1997), 7.

4. While birth years for each generation can vary, these numbers are based

on Pew Research Center's divisions in "The generations defined," April 11, 2018, www.pewresearch.org.

5. "Stradivarius Violins," Smithsonian, accessed July 12, 2018, www.si.edu.

6. Wendy Powers, "Violin Makers: Nicolò Amati (1596–1684) and Antonio Stradivari (1644–1737)," The Metropolitan Museum of Art, October 2003, www.metmuseum.org.

7. Special thanks to Chris Forbes, et al., for permission to print from *Hidden Harvest: Discovering Oklahoma's Unchurched* (Baptist General Convention of Oklahoma, 2018).

CHAPTER 5

1. Dave Chaffey, "Global social media research summary 2018," Smart Insights, March 28, 2018, www.smartinsights.com.

2. While many studies cite multiple downfalls of social media use, here's another example for further investigation: Neal Samudre, "8 Dangers of Social Media We're Not Willing to Admit" *Relevant*, April 19, 2016, https://relevantmagazine.com.

3. For more information on "Isonection," see Dr. Ron Hannaford's discussion on "Social Media in Education: Connection or Isonection," Biola Digital Media Conference 2013, June 5, 2013, http://open.biola.edu/resources/social-media-in-education-connection-or-isonection.

CHAPTER 6

1. Beth Moore, as quoted on Twitter, June 18, 2018, @BethMooreLPM.

CHAPTER 7

1. John Ortberg, *Everybody's Normal Till You Get to Know Them* (Grand Rapids, MI: Zondervan, 2003), 44.

2. Ibid, 47.

3. Ibid.

4. Don Carson, as quoted in Matt Smethurst, "6 Pillars of a Christian View on Suffering," The Gospel Coalition, June 2, 2013, www.thegospelcoalition.org.

5. Kaye Hurta, "The Language of Grief," LifeWay Christian Resources, April 6, 2018, www.lifeway.com/womensministry.

6. Daryl Crouch, "Four guidelines for mental health issues and the church," The Ethics & Religious Liberty Commission of the Southern Baptist Convention, February 16, 2018, https://erlc.com.

CHAPTER 8

1. David Geisler and Norman Geisler, *Conversational Evangelism: Connecting with People to Share Jesus* (Eugene, Oregon: Harvest House Publishing, 2009), 28.

2. Selma Wilson, "4 Dangers of Not Listening," as quoted on the LifeWay Leadership Blog, March 8, 2017, https://leadership.lifeway.com.

3. Ibid, Geisler, 46.

4. One of my current favorite ways to present the gospel is the "3 Circles" presentation. You can find it online at lifeonmissionbook.com or download the app on your smartphone. It will walk you through seeing three areas: God's design, our brokenness, and how the gospel is available to anyone who repents and believes.

5. Steve Hawthorne and Graham Kendrick, *Prayerwalking: Praying On Site with Insight* (Lake Mary, FL: Charisma House, 1993), 12.

CHAPTER 9

1. "The Scriptures," *The Baptist Faith and Message,* The Southern Baptist Convention, accessed July 19, 2018, www.sbc.net.

2. Selma Wilson, "The Boy's Table: Leading Alongside Men," September 3, 2014, www.selmawilson.com.

3. "Spiritual Gifts Survey," © 2003 LifeWay Christian Resources. Reprinted with permission. You have permission to make copies of this survey for distribution within your women's ministry.

RESOURCES BY CHAPTER

CHAPTER 3—Making Disciples: The Heart of Your Ministry to Women

Names of God

While this is not an exhaustive list of the names of God found in Scripture, these are some of the more common descriptions of God's character, as compiled in the *Experiencing God Bible Study,* by Henry and Richard Blackaby and Claude King. They might help when trying to add variety to group prayer times.

☐ "Source and perfecter of our faith"	Hebrews 12:2
☐ "Bread of life"	John 6:48
☐ "Creator of heaven and earth"	Genesis 14:19
☐ "Father of the fatherless"	Psalm 68:5
☐ "Champion of widows"	Psalm 68:5
☐ "Faithful and True"	Revelation 19:11
☐ "Helper of the fatherless"	Psalm 10:14
☐ "Immanuel, ... God with us"	Matthew 1:23
☐ "Jealous"	Exodus 20:5
☐ "KING OF KINGS AND LORD OF LORDS"	Revelation 19:16
☐ "Light of the world"	John 8:12
☐ "My Lord, my strong Savior"	Psalm 140:7
☐ "Prince of Peace"	Isaiah 9:6
☐ "Shepherd"	Psalm 23:1
☐ "The way, the truth, and the life"	John 14:6
☐ "Wonderful Counselor"	Isaiah 9:6

CHAPTER 5—Communication: Can You Hear Me Now?

Looking for help generating social media posts and images can be tricky. We recommend the following apps, if you need a good starting place:

☐ BOOMERANG
☐ LIVELY
☐ REPOST
☐ SNAPSEED
☐ STOREO
☐ WORDSWAG

PULL UP A CHAIR.

Drop by the LifeWay Women blog to grow in your faith, develop as a leader, and find encouragement as you go. Find inside info on Bible studies, events near you, giveaways, and more at

LIFEWAYWOMEN.COM

LifeWay | Women

TRAIN WITH KELLY KING LIVE

LifeWay Women's LEADERSHIP FORUM

Equipping Every Woman for God's Call

Get equipped to lead with three days of intensive training, including teaching from top authors and ministry leaders and breakout sessions for personalized development.

Learn More at LifeWay.com/WomensForum

You LEAD

GROWING EVERY WOMAN'S LEADERSHIP POTENTIAL

Learn through efficient, one-day regional training events across the country before select Living Proof Live and Going Beyond Live events.

Find a City Near You at LifeWay.com/YouLead

LifeWay Women | events

To register by phone, call 800.254.2022. Events subject to change without notice.

SPACE
IS
AWESOME!

101 INCREDIBLE THINGS EVERY KID SHOULD KNOW

ALICE HARMAN

ARCTURUS

Picture credits

p15tr: Nima Kasraie; p28tl NASA/Robert Markowitz; p33t U.S. Army; p33b Draper Laboratory, restored by Adam Cuerden; p34 NASA/JPL; p35tr National Astronomy and Ionosphere Center; p38 USGov-NASA; p39m NASA; p41b NASA; p42t NASA; p43m Maksym Kozlenko; p45b Johan Hagemeyer; p47m NASA; p52t Ken Crawford; p57b John Colosimo/ESO; p59b NASA/CXC/Huntingdon Inst. for X-ray Astronomy/G. Garmire, ESO/VLT; p65t Denys; p66t Smithsonian Institution; p73m The Yerkes Observatory; p102t NASA/JPL-Caltech/MSSS; p106t NASA/JPL-Caltech; p107m N. Metcalfe & Pan-STARRS 1 Science Consortium; p109t NASA; p112b NASA, H. Ford (JHU), G. Illingworth (UCSC/LO), M.Clampin (STScI), G. Hartig (STScI), the ACS Science Team, and ESA; p113b University of Warwick/Mark Garlick; p114t ESA/Hubble & NASA Acknowledgment: Judy Schmidt; p115t NASA/ESA/Hubble Heritage Team; p115b NASA Goddard Space Flight Center; p117b ESO; p119t NASA/JPL-Caltech; p119b NASA/CXC/Stanford/I. Zhuravleva et al. All other images from Shutterstock.

ARCTURUS

This edition published in 2019 by Arcturus Publishing Limited
26/27 Bickels Yard, 151–153 Bermondsey Street,
London SE1 3HA

Copyright © Arcturus Holdings Limited

Author: Alice Harman
Editor: Becca Clunes
Designer: Sarah Fountain

978-1-78950-031-8
CH006565NT
Supplier 26, Date 0319, Print run 7963

Printed in China

What is STEM?

STEM is a world-wide initiative that aims to cultivate an interest in Science, Technology, Engineering, and Mathematics, in an effort to promote these disciplines to as wide a variety of students as possible.

Introduction

SPACE IS AMAZING!

From the Sun in the sky all day to the Moon and stars at night, space is a part of our everyday life. But sometimes we can take it for granted, rather than stopping to think about just how incredible it is! In this book you'll find 101 amazing facts about space—everything from animal astronauts and exploding stars to cannibal galaxies and diamond rain.

What does space smell like? Why could crying in space kill you? How does our atmosphere protect us from asteroids? All of these questions and many more will be answered in the pages of this book, so read on and open your eyes to the mind-blowing world of space!

FACT 1

YOU LIVE INSIDE THE SUN!

Earth is inside the Sun's atmosphere, the layer of gases that surround the burning star. In fact, the whole of our solar system sits within the Sun's atmosphere.

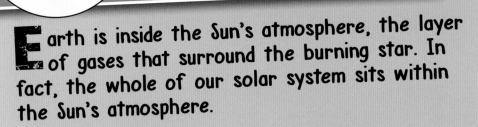

Layers of atmosphere

The Sun's atmosphere is made up of three layers. The layer closest to the Sun's surface is the photosphere, and it's so bright that usually it's the only part of the Sun we can see. Next comes the chromosphere. The gases in this layer get hotter and hotter as they move out, reaching around 9,700°C (17,500°F). But that's nothing compared to the outermost layer, the corona ...

FACT 2

The Sun makes up more than 99% of the mass of the solar system. Jupiter makes up most of the rest.

The mighty corona

The corona is around 200 to 500 times hotter than the chromosphere layer below it, reaching up to 3 million Celsius (5.4 million Fahrenheit). The corona stretches around 5 million km (3 million miles) into space, and then turns into the solar wind, the Sun's flowing atmosphere that stretches across the solar system. Earth is within the reach of this solar wind, but luckily it cools down a lot before it gets to us!

Magnetic power

The corona's extreme heat might be linked to the fact that the Sun is powerfully magnetic. Electric currents within the Sun create a magnetic field that affects our entire solar system. One of the things this field does is protect us from 90% of the deadly cosmic rays moving through space. The amount of radiation that makes it through to Earth is low enough not to cause us problems.

The corona

Earth

Sun

Earth's magnetic field

Solar winds

Space weather

Changes in the Sun's magnetic field, such as powerful magnetic storms, can affect us on Earth. The Sun shoots out solar winds, streams of speeding energy particles that can overcome Earth's own magnetic field and make our electronic objects stop working properly.

The Northern and Southern Lights occur when solar winds hit the Earth's atmosphere.

5

FACT 3
YOU ARE ALWAYS MOVING AT SUPER SPEED

Even when you're just sitting on the sofa watching TV, you're actually moving very fast! The Earth travels 970 million km (600 million miles) around the Sun each year.

Wheeeeee!!

Tied to the Sun

The Sun is much bigger than Earth, so it has much stronger gravity. The Sun pulls on Earth, so rather than Earth free-floating through space it is tied to the Sun and constantly travels around it in a set path. This is called Earth's orbit around the Sun, and it is more of a stretched egg shape than a perfect circle. The other planets in the solar system are also trapped orbiting around the Sun.

AROUND 1,300,000 EARTHS COULD FIT INSIDE THE SUN.

Spinning around

At the same time as Earth is moving around the Sun, it is also constantly spinning around. From here on Earth, it looks like the Sun is moving up and down and across the sky through the day. It's like when you look out of the window on a fast train and everything outside seems to be speeding past, but actually it is the train that is moving rather than anything outside.

Good night, Sun! We'll spin around and see you again tomorrow.

Star safari

As Earth orbits the Sun, it travels through different areas of space and we can see different stars. Earth always moves in the same direction around the Sun and at roughly the same speed, so we know which stars and other objects in space we will be able to see at certain times of the year.

FACT 4

If a human ran as fast as Earth moves around the Sun, they would finish seven back-to-back marathons in a single second.

Chain of orbits

The Sun does not stay still while Earth and the other planets in our solar system move around it. It orbits the middle point of our galaxy, the Milky Way, at around 230 km (143 miles) a second. The Milky Way orbits around a point between itself and the largest nearby galaxy, Andromeda. And our entire Local Group of galaxies orbits within a larger group called the Virgo Supercluster, which itself moves around other bigger structures. It's exhausting!

FACT 5

MORE THAN 1,300 EARTHS WOULD FIT INSIDE JUPITER

The Moon is a long way from Earth, around 384,400 km (238,900 miles). If you lined up all the planets in our solar system end to end, they could fit in the space between Earth and the Moon.

The little ones

The four inner planets in the solar system—Mercury, Venus, Earth, and Mars—don't take up very much space at all. Mercury is the smallest planet, and could fit inside Earth 18 times over. Scientists think that some of Mercury's surface might have been burned off when it was forming, because of it being so close to the Sun. Its huge liquid metal core makes up 75% of its total size, which is unusual for a planet.

Jump in Mercury, there's lots of room!

8

The frozen giants

It's a big jump in size from the inner planets to the outer frozen giants. Jupiter and Saturn are gas giant planets, while Neptune and Uranus are ice giants. Neptune and Uranus are around four times the size of Earth, but Uranus is a little bigger than Neptune. Neptune is a bit heavier than Uranus, though, because of the different materials in its core.

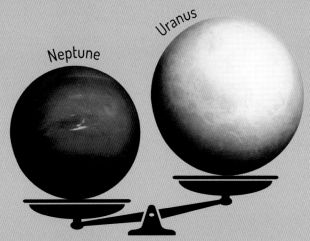

Neptune

Uranus

The big players

The planet taking up the most space by far in this line-up would be Jupiter. It is so big that all the other planets in the solar system could fit inside it with plenty of room to spare. Saturn is the second largest planet in our solar system and, like Jupiter, it is called a gas giant. Gas giants have a small, rocky core but are mostly made up of layers of liquid and gas.

Speeding through space

Despite the huge distance between Earth and the Moon, it only takes about three days for a spacecraft to travel there! A spacecraft has to be going very fast to break away from Earth's gravity and out into space—around 11 km (7 miles) a second, which means a speedy journey to the Moon. The Moon is working against us, though ... it's moving 3.82 cm (1.5 inches) farther away from Earth each year!

FACT 6

OUR HOTTEST PLANET IS NOT CLOSEST TO THE SUN

Mercury may be the closest planet to the Sun, but it's fiery Venus that takes the top hot spot in our solar system. The second planet from the Sun is a meltingly hot 462°C (864°F).

Hell on Venus

Venus can often be seen with the naked eye from Earth. Looking at this beautiful, bright planet shining in the sky, you'd never know how hellish it is down on its surface. As well as being burning hot, it also has such thick clouds of acid that almost no sunlight gets through, making it a dark and gloomy place. Add in its raging winds, wild storms, volcanoes, and crushing air pressure and it's not looking very appealing ...

I'm hot stuff!

FACT 7

Venus's hurricanes are over twice as fast as the strongest hurricanes on Earth.

Locking in heat

Venus's atmosphere, the layer of gases that surround planets, is mainly made of carbon dioxide. Venus is hot because of the "greenhouse effect" created by carbon dioxide, which traps a lot of the Sun's heat and only lets a small amount of it back out into space again. This is also happening on Earth and causing global warming.

Rays

Heat

Moon-like Mercury

Over on Mercury (below), it's a bit calmer than on Venus. In fact, it looks very much like the Moon! Mercury's surface is also rocky and covered with craters . Another similarity between Mercury and the Moon is that they both have only a very, very thin atmosphere. As the closest planet, Mercury gets a lot of heat from the Sun, but almost all of it quickly escapes back into space again.

Too hot and too cold!

It is still incredibly hot on Mercury at times, though. When it faces the Sun, Mercury's surface can reach 427°C (801°F)—almost as hot as Venus. But when it spins away from the Sun and night falls, the temperature can get as cold as -180°C (-290°F). The hottest and coldest temperatures ever recorded on Earth are 56.7°C (134°F) and –89.2 °C (-128.6 °F).

PLUTO IS ONLY HALF AS WIDE AS THE USA

Poor Pluto. It used to be considered the ninth planet in our solar system, but scientists have realized that it's just too small to be a real planet.

Days of glory

For 76 years, Pluto was part of an elite group—the planets of our solar system. First discovered in 1930, it was believed to be the most distant planet from the Sun. But in 2006 scientists decided it isn't a planet after all. It meets the first two "musts" of being a planet—circling a star (the Sun) and having enough gravity to pull itself into a round 3D shape—but fails the final test ...

THE LARGEST OF PLUTO'S FIVE MOONS, CHARON, IS SO BIG THAT IT MAKES PLUTO WOBBLE.

USA

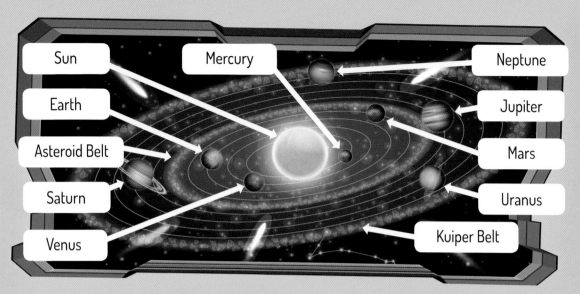

Sun · Mercury · Neptune · Earth · Jupiter · Asteroid Belt · Mars · Saturn · Uranus · Venus · Kuiper Belt

Sharing space

Pluto hasn't managed to clear the area around it of other objects, which is the third thing a planet needs to do. It is part of the Kuiper Belt, an area of icy objects on the outskirts of our solar system, and it still shares its space with a number of other large objects. It is too small to have strong enough gravity to either trap large nearby objects in its gravity or to throw them out into space.

Tough decisions

There was a lot of global debate between scientists before Pluto was downgraded from a planet to a dwarf planet. If scientists had allowed Pluto to be considered a planet despite only meeting two out of the three standards, other objects in our solar system—including many moons —would also have to be considered planets. We could have ended up with dozens of official planets—that's a lot of names to remember!

FACT
9

Several moons in our solar system are larger than the dwarf planets, but can't be dwarf planets because they orbit a planet themselves.

Dwarf planets

At the moment, Pluto is one of five official dwarf planets in our solar system. Three of the other dwarf planets—Haumea, Makemake, and Eris—are near Pluto, in the Kuiper Belt. Ceres is the only dwarf planet in the asteroid belt, between Mars and Jupiter. Scientists believe there are many more dwarf planets in our solar system that we haven't yet discovered—up to 200 in the Kuiper Belt and 10,000 in the area beyond.

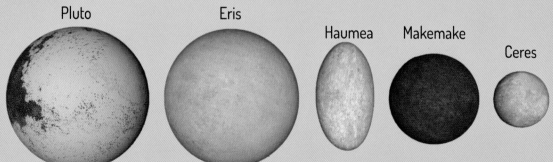

Pluto · Eris · Haumea · Makemake · Ceres

13

FACT 10

THE MOON MAY HAVE BEEN PART OF EARTH

Many scientists believe that the Moon is made from material chipped off the Earth when an object the size of Mars crashed into our young planet around 4.45 billion years ago.

Violent beginnings

That long ago, Earth would only have been around 50 million years old and the solar system would also only recently have come together. In these early stages, big crashes are very common. Many scientists think that the huge amounts of hot, rocky material blown off Earth by this crash got trapped by Earth's gravity and circled around the Earth, eventually clumping together to create the Moon.

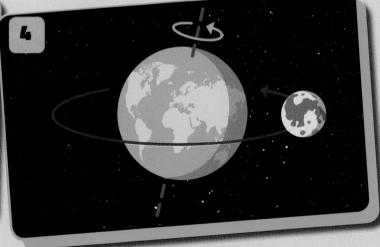

The Big Splash theory

This Moon creation story is often called the "Big Splash" theory. It fits with some things we have learned about the Moon. Astronauts have collected rock samples from the Moon which are similar in some ways to rocks found on Earth. Also, the Moon doesn't have much iron compared to Earth, but most of Earth's iron is in its core so if the Moon is made of its rocky outer layer this would make sense.

This moon rock was collected during the Apollo 15 mission in 1971.

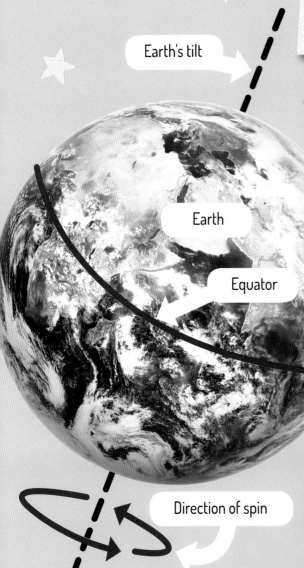

Earth's tilt

Earth

Equator

Direction of spin

Other Moon theories

It's important to remember that scientists do not always agree on a single theory, although often one idea becomes more popular than others over time. Some scientists still believe that the Moon is one huge chunk chipped off the Earth, rather than lots of bits of material that later joined together. Others think that it was a large passing object that was trapped in Earth's gravity when it got too close.

Tilted Earth

Imagine grabbing a pole in a fire station and swinging around and around on it in one direction. Earth constantly spins like this around its axis, an imaginary pole running through its middle. Except its axis doesn't stand up exactly straight—it tilts a bit to one side. It is widely thought that this is because when the large object hit Earth and created the Moon, the force of it also knocked the Earth permanently off kilter.

FACT 11 EARTH HAS A SECOND (MINI) MOON

The asteroid 2016 HO3 is circling Earth like the Moon we all know and love, and has probably been doing so for the last 100 years.

Get out! I'm the only real Moon.

Shhh, I just want a nice family picture.

EARTH'S MOON IS UNUSUALLY LARGE COMPARED TO OUR PLANET'S SIZE.

A sort-of moon

Asteroid 2016 HO3 is not exactly a true moon, as it drifts a little behind or ahead of Earth as it circles our planet. Another name for a moon is a natural satellite—it orbits around a planet like man-made satellites for weather and TV do. 2016 HO3 is a quasi-satellite—in other words, a sort-of moon—because it doesn't stick close enough to Earth.

16

Dancing with Earth

Although asteroid 2016 HO3 is around 100 times farther away from Earth than the Moon, and doesn't stick as closely to us, it definitely has a long-term connection to Earth. It will be with us for centuries to come. Other asteroids sometimes get trapped in Earth's gravity and, as NASA puts it, "dance with Earth" for a while, but only for a short time and then they are back off on their way.

No-moon mystery

Neither Mercury nor Venus has a moon. Mercury doesn't have a moon because it is so close to the Sun that its own gravity could never compete with the Sun's pull. It is more of a mystery as to why Venus doesn't have a moon. Many scientists think it's still too close to the Sun, some think its moon was destroyed, and others think that it "gave" Earth a moon. How generous!

The pattern 2016 HO3 makes when it circles the Earth is unusual.

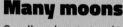
FACT 12
Ganymede and Titan, Jupiter's and Saturn's largest moons, are both bigger than Mercury.

Many moons

Smaller planets tend to have few or no moons whereas larger planets can have huge numbers of them. Scientists think that Jupiter has 79 known moons in total, the highest number in our solar system, although only 53 have been officially named so far. Twelve of the planet's moons were only discovered for the first time in 2017.

JUPITER PROTECTS US FROM DEADLY COMETS

Some scientists believe that one reason we are able to live on Earth is because Jupiter's strong gravity helps to pull fast-moving comets away from Earth and throw them back out of our solar system.

Giant protectors

With Jupiter's help these really fast comets only hit Earth very rarely, every few millions or even tens of millions of years. Without Jupiter nearby, some scientists believe that comets would crash into Earth far more often. There are other scientists who think that Saturn also plays a big a role in protecting Earth, and that it's only the combined force of Jupiter's and Saturn's gravity which is strong enough to make a difference.

COMETS ARE MADE OF ICE, DUST, AND ROCK WHILE ASTEROIDS ARE USUALLY MADE OF METAL AND ROCK.

Leave my friend alone!

Thanks, Jupiter.

FACT 14

The first crash seen between two natural objects in space was Comet Shoemaker–Levy 9 hitting Jupiter in 1994.

Scars on Jupiter

Although Jupiter may play a role in protecting Earth from speeding comets, space objects such as comets and asteroids crash into Jupiter very often. When Comet Shoemaker-Levy 9 smashed into Jupiter, its pieces created dark scars on the planet's surface that were visible from Earth. In 2009 a dark spot the size of Earth was seen on Jupiter, believed to be damage caused by an asteroid only around 500 m (550 yards) wide.

Everyday scientists

Amateur astronomers—people who are not professional scientists but enjoy looking at and learning about space—have seen many objects crash into Jupiter in recent years. If seen in real time, this looks like a big "flash" of light, and the time it lasts tells us how large and heavy the object is. Amateurs' photos and videos are very useful, as professional telescopes don't always happen to be looking in the right place at the right time.

Asteroid crashes

While Jupiter often protects Earth from crashes, its strong gravity can sometimes work against us and send the occasional space object speeding in our direction instead—yikes! Some scientists believe Jupiter may have played a role in sending a huge asteroid to Earth 66 million years ago and killing off the dinosaurs, which let mammals grow and humans eventually evolve.

Dinosaurs may have been killed off by an asteroid crashing into Earth.

OUR SOLAR SYSTEM IS MIDDLE AGED

Our solar system is about halfway through its (very long) life. Scientists think our solar system began around 4.6 billion years ago and will survive for another 5 billion years.

Wow, that's an old rock!

This meteorite fell to Earth near Buenos Aires, Argentina.

Radioactive dating

So how do scientists know how old the solar system is in the first place? They can find out the age of ancient rocks and meteorites by looking at how radioactive materials in them have broken down over time. Radioactive materials give out radiation and break down very predictably, so scientists can work backward from their current state to tell their age. The oldest meteorites from our solar system that have ever been dated are 4.56 billion years old.

Running out of fuel

The Sun burns up its stores of hydrogen as fuel to survive. So far it has used about half of its hydrogen, so it has another 5 billion years' worth. Once it has burned up all this hydrogen, it will have to use its other materials for fuel and then it will begin to die.

A giant Sun

As the Sun dies it will get much, much bigger and hotter, becoming a red giant star. It will grow out to reach Earth, perhaps farther, probably destroying our planet as well as Mercury and Venus. Some scientists believe that Earth might instead be pushed out into space rather than burned up by the Sun. Either way, by this time Earth will be way too hot to support life.

Life after Earth

As the Sun grows into a red giant, and planets and moons farther out in our solar system grow warmer, life may be possible there for a while. As the Sun then shrinks and becomes a white dwarf, these planets will continue circling the Sun's cold, dim remains for a long time. Scientists are searching for planets outside our solar system that may be able to support human life in future.

LIFE MAY BE POSSIBLE ON OTHER PLANETS' MOONS

For a long time, scientists concentrated on finding other planets that may support alien life. Now, they are equally concerned about whether other planets could support humans.

Saturn and its sixth-largest moon, Enceladus.

Living on a moon

Jupiter and Saturn have lots of moons, and scientists believe that life may be able to evolve on some of them. We may think of our Moon as a cold, empty place compared to Earth, but if humans need to leave Earth in future, a moon might be our best option. With the help of advanced technology, we may be able to create an environment in which we can survive there.

FACT 17

Jupiter's moons Io, Ganymede, Europa, and Calisto are so big you can see them with just a pair of binoculars.

We don't know what aliens might look like, but it's unlikely they'll be like in the movies!

Moon oceans

Saturn's moon Enceladus and Jupiter's moon Europa both have liquid water oceans under their frozen surfaces. Saturn's moon Titan has an ocean of liquid methane (a gas on Earth) rather than water. Although scientists don't think this methane ocean could support any life forms familiar to us, it's possible that very different life forms could evolve in space and survive in this kind of environment.

Alien life

Scientists are hopeful enough about the possibility of life forms existing on Europa that a team once purposely destroyed a satellite heading toward Europa to stop it crash-landing and possibly hurting alien life. The Cassini spacecraft has recently explored Enceladus and found conditions in its oceans similar to those that we believe led to early life on Earth.

THE SEARCH FOR EXTRATERRESTRIAL LIFE IS OFTEN SHORTENED TO "SETI."

Better off on Earth

As far as we know, Earth is the only planet that is perfectly suited for humans to live on—as long as we treat it with respect. We need to stop global warming so we aren't forced off Earth before we have the technology to survive elsewhere. Positive change is possible! We've already shrunk the hole in the ozone layer—a part of our atmosphere that protects us from the sun's heat—just by stopping using certain chemicals.

FACT 18 CRYING IN SPACE COULD KILL YOU

Your eyes can form tears in space, but because there is no gravity the tears won't fall. They just make a big liquid bubble on your face. This can be very bad news ...

Dangerous tears

Andrew Feustel found out the hard way how risky crying in space can be. While he was on a spacewalk outside the International Space Station, a flake of the solution used to defog the inside of his spacesuit helmet got in his eye. It stung, so his eye reacted naturally and started watering to try to flush out the irritation. But crying doesn't work like that in space.

FACT 19 Astronauts wear normal clothes in space, and only put on a spacesuit when they walk outside the spacecraft.

Nooo, I can't see!

Blinded in space

As Andrew's eye pushed out tears, a liquid bubble formed and spread across his face and into his other eye. The tears stung painfully and meant he couldn't see anything at all, but there was very little anyone could do. Which is not what you want to hear when, as Andrew was, you are floating in space holding a power drill.

Happy ending

Luckily, after some time, Andrew eventually managed to move inside his spacesuit to rub his eye on a sticking-out piece of foam. He finished his spacewalk and returned safely to the International Space Station (ISS). Inside the ISS astronauts don't have to wear spacesuits with helmets, so although tears bubble on your face in the same way it's less of an issue as you can use your hands to brush them away. You can even watch them float in front of you!

WE HAVE TEARS IN OUR EYES ALL THE TIME TO KEEP THEM MOIST—THEY ARE CALLED BASAL TEARS.

Microgravity

The reason that tears do not fall inside or outside the ISS is not because there is no gravity. In fact, the ISS is so close to Earth that it still has 90% gravity. The reason is microgravity—the same reason you feel like you're flying just as a rollercoaster drops downward. As gravity pulls the ISS toward Earth, other forces pull it sideways, so rather than crashing down to Earth it free-falls around our planet in a constant circle.

25

FACT 20

SPACE SMELLS LIKE STEAK AND BURNING METAL

Astronauts agree that space smells ... funny. People describe it differently, but most agree that it is at once sweet, sharp, and metallic.

Bringing in a smell

Have you ever brought anything smelly into the house on your shoes? Don't worry, so have astronauts! Astronaut Don Pettit has said that his fellow astronauts carried in a "space smell" with them when they returned from spacewalks. Whenever he opened the hatch on the spacecraft to bring the astronauts back in, he noticed their spacesuits, gloves, helmets, and even their tools smelled odd—but it took him a while to figure out why!

SCIENTISTS BELIEVE HUMANS CAN RECOGNIZE 1 TRILLION DIFFERENT SMELLS.

Sugar and rotten eggs

Our solar system may be especially smelly. We have lots of carbon in our solar system and not much oxygen, giving it a strong and sooty smell. Think of an old car that gives off lots of nasty smoke from its exhaust—nice! We could have it worse—solar systems with lots of sulfur may smell like rotten eggs. On the other hand, it could be better, as scientists think some solar systems smell sugary sweet!

Eugh, who would have thought our solar system stunk like an old car?!

Astronaut smells

With up to six living, breathing human beings living aboard the International Space Station at any one time, things could get a bit smelly. Especially as no-one can have a shower or do laundry properly in space. There is a good built-in system for clearing smells but astronauts have said they sometimes got annoyed with each other for leaving sweaty workout clothes around and cooking smelly food!

Smell science

NASA has thought about trying to recreate the smell of space on Earth, talking to scientists about how they might be able to do this. The reason isn't just their curiosity—going into space is an exciting but often overwhelming experience, so in NASA's training programme they try to prepare people as fully as they can for their trip. This includes recreating sights, sounds, and maybe even smells.

FACT
21

You can't do laundry in space so dirty clothes are destroyed. They are sent down to Earth in a disposable spacecraft that burns up in the atmosphere, over the ocean.

SPACE TRAVEL CAN CHANGE YOUR BODY FOREVER

Astronaut Scott Kelly spent a year in the International Space Station. When he came back, scientists found that some interesting changes had taken place inside his body.

Scott and Mark Kelly

Twin astronauts

Scott Kelly has an identical twin brother, Mark, who is also an astronaut. As their DNA is almost identical, scientists can run some very interesting experiments looking at how each brother's DNA is affected by experiences in space. After Scott spent a year in space, many newspaper reports said his DNA had changed so much that he and Mark—who had remained on Earth—were no longer identical. It's a great headline but it's not quite right ...

FACT
23

Space can cause astronauts' eyes to change in ways that can cause vision problems and possibly even blindness.

Do I look different?

Switching genes

Genes are segments of our DNA, the code written into our body's cells that describe how we look and many other things about us. We inherit our genes from our parents, but different conditions or events in our lives can cause them to "switch" on and off and affect our body in different ways. What you eat, where you live, when you sleep, and all sorts of other things can trigger these on/off changes.

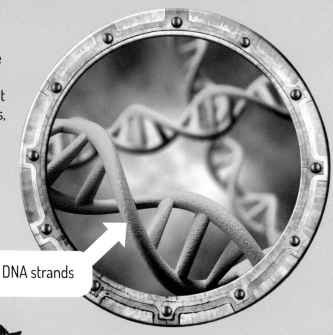

DNA strands

Permanent change

As you might imagine, going into space is quite an unusual thing for a person to do. However exciting it may be, it also puts a lot of physical stress on the body. It can cause genes to switch on and off, sometimes permanently so. While Scott was in space and Mark remained on Earth, Scott's genes switched on and off in different ways and it looks like around 7% of these changes are irreversible.

Bodies in space

Other changes are temporary— for instance, scientists found that Scott was taller than when he'd left, because the lower gravity in space meant his spine wasn't pulled down toward Earth as much. This happens to everyone in space, and they usually return to their pre-space height within ten days.

FACT 24 ASTRONAUTS CAN TIME TRAVEL

Time moves faster in space than on Earth because the Earth's orbit gives us an extra second per week. This means astronauts time travel as they move between space and Earth.

Space clocks

The existence of this extra time on Earth is called "time dilation" and it has been proven over and over again by taking very accurate clocks on trips into space. We can compare the time on two clocks—one in space and one on Earth—and see the difference between them. Scientists have also recorded the time difference between a pair of clocks after one of them had been in space.

I want my 100 millionths of a second back!

Einstein time

Famous scientist Albert Einstein "realized" that time isn't always the same—it depends on where you are. This isn't just true for space, though. Being higher up on Earth also means that you experience time as faster. If you spent your whole life at the top of a 100-floor skyscraper, you would lose around 100 millionths of a second of your life. Scientists have used clocks that are accurate to within one second over 3.7 billion years to show this on Earth.

Travel to the future

Russian cosmonaut Sergei Krikalev has spent more time orbiting around the Earth than anyone else—a total of 803 days, 9 hours and 39 minutes. This means he's completed more time travel than anyone else on Earth. As he still lives in the same time frame as everyone else on Earth, it is as if he has gone 0.02 seconds into his own future.

Science fiction

Along with invisibility and being able to fly, time travel is something that many people would love to do. But is it possible on a larger scale—days, months, years? Many scientists think so, although it's much more complicated to think about how to travel into the past than into the future. We are still only beginning to understand how things work differently elsewhere in space compared to on Earth, and what incredible things that might make possible.

A trip to the past? Maybe some day ...

FACT 25

YOUR PHONE COULD POWER THE MOON LANDING

Smartphones today are far more powerful than the supercomputers of the past which launched rockets into space in the 1960s and put men on the Moon.

Genius phones

A smartphone is an incredible piece of technology. It does the job of an address book, a calculator, an alarm clock, a map, a music player, a payment card, a bus ticket, and so many more things. It's not just a phone, it's a brilliantly fast and versatile computer that we carry around in our pocket—and it performs instructions hundreds of million times faster than the best computers used in the Apollo Moon missions.

> Texting? Don't you know I could send you to space?!

Back in time

It's easy to forget that when we first landed on the Moon in 1969, the very first general-purpose programmable electronic computer had only been completed 23 years earlier. It was called ENIAC and the USA began building it during World War II. It eventually took up around 167 sq m (1800 sq ft) of space—that makes it the size of seven buses! It weighed around 30 tons, as much as five elephants.

Faster, stronger, smarter

By the time of the first Apollo space missions in the 1960s computers were more advanced, and they kept evolving over the following decades. As we moved into the new millennium, though, this rate of development kicked up to turbo speed. Technology has developed so quickly that even "smart" refrigerators and microwaves have more computing power than any of the computers NASA used to help put people on the Moon, let alone our smartphones!

Super programmers

The usefulness of a computer isn't just about its raw power, though—it depends on programmers working out how to give the computer its instructions. Margaret Hamilton, a NASA programmer on the Apollo missions, has said that it was like working in the "Wild West"—there weren't really many rules yet, they just had to make it up and try it! These programmers' genius and creativity helped harness the computers' limited power to do incredible things.

Margaret Hamilton and the software that powered the Apollo project.

FACT 26

WE HAVE SENT OUT MESSAGES FOR ALIENS

The Voyager I spacecraft was launched in 1977 with a solid gold record on board. It plays sounds from Earth and is intended as a friendly introduction for aliens who find it.

Introducing Earth

If you had to introduce an alien to life on Earth, which sights and sounds would you choose to give them the best possible understanding of our planet? The people responsible for the Golden Record had to decide exactly this. No pressure! A committee put together by NASA and headed by famous scientist Carl Sagan worked together to choose the contents—a selection of images, music, sounds from Earth, and greetings in different languages.

FACT 27

The Golden Record has a recording of a woman's brainwaves as she thought about subjects including history, the Earth's problems, and what it is like to fall in love.

Hello! We are from Earth!

Wie gehts?

Cover art

The record cover has a number of diagrams on one side, explaining where the spacecraft comes from and how the record can be played. As you would hope, NASA thought to include a record player on board so that any aliens can actually play it! There are also 115 images encoded onto the record itself—including photos of a city at night, heavy traffic on a road, and people eating or drinking in different ways.

THE GOLDEN RECORD IS DESIGNED TO STILL BE PLAYABLE A BILLION YEARS FROM NOW.

One of the images on the Golden Record, showing people eating and drinking— a bit strangely!

Earth sounds

Aliens playing the record will first hear a number of human greetings—starting in an ancient language called Akkadian and finishing in a modern Chinese dialect called Wu. The sounds of Earth include a human heartbeat, a baby crying, a train, and a dog barking. After this comes a 90-minute selection of music from all over the world—including classical Western and Eastern music, traditional songs from indigenous communities, rock 'n' roll, and the blues.

Swinging through space

The Voyager I (left) and Voyager II spacecraft were launched in the 1970s to take advantage of planets in our solar system lining up in a way that only happens every 176 years. The spacecraft used the gravity of each planet to swing to the next and eventually study our solar system's outer planets. After leaving our solar system they will travel through mostly empty space for a very long time—but we hope aliens may come across them some day ...

NEW PLANETS ARE DISCOVERED ALMOST EVERY DAY

Back in 1994, scientists Michel Mayor and Didier Queloz found a planet outside our solar system—but people didn't believe them for almost a year! Now we have found thousands, with more discovered all the time.

Exoplanets

An exoplanet is what we call a planet outside our solar system. Exoplanets circle around other stars, just as Earth circles around the Sun. Although no exoplanets were found until the 1990s, scientists had believed for years before this time that they existed. The reason behind this belief was that in understanding how planets formed around our Sun scientists realized that planets would similarly form around other Sun-like stars.

An artist's impression of 51 Pegasi b circling a star.

Too big

So if scientists believed in exoplanets, why did it take them so long to be convinced by the two scientists' 1994 discovery? Well, the issue was that this planet, named 51 Pegasi b—the first ever found circling around a Sun-like star—was just too big. The existence of an exoplanet this size didn't fit with scientists' ideas at the time about how planets were formed, so they thought at first that it must be a mistake.

I'm looking for a Goldilocks planet!

Goldilocks planets

The powerful telescopes available today help with spotting exoplanets. One focus of this search is finding "Goldilocks planets," named after the fairy tale. Like Goldilocks searching through the bears' house, scientists are trying to find a planet that is not too hot, not too cold, but just right for life to exist there.

FACT
29

The first evidence of an exoplanet was noted in 1917 ... but it was not recognized as a planet at the time.

Not the first

51 Pegasi b was the first exoplanet to be discovered orbiting a Sun-like star, but it was not the first exoplanet to be discovered. In 1992, Aleksander Wolszczan and Dale Frail found exoplanets around a type of tiny, fast-spinning star called a pulsar, which is the squeezed core left over after a massive star explodes.

FACT 30 FOOTPRINTS ON THE MOON STAY THERE FOREVER

There is no water or wind on the Moon to sweep away footprints on its surface. This means that astronauts' footprints may last as long as the Moon itself.

FACT 31 The word astronaut comes from the Greek word "astron" (star) and "nautes" (sailor).

Walking on the Moon

Twenty-four people have flown to the Moon and twelve people have actually walked on its surface. The most famous are the first two to walk on the Moon's surface: Neil Armstrong and Buzz Aldrin. They flew there on the Apollo 11 mission, first stepping out onto the Moon on July 20, 1969. They spent over 21 hours on its surface, but less than three hours outside of the landing spacecraft.

Just look at all these footprints!

Moon littering

It isn't just footprints that humans have left on the Moon. For a start, there are hundreds of pieces of spacecraft wreckage. Visiting astronauts have also left things behind, including two golf balls; 12 pairs of boots; empty food packets; 12 cameras (the films were brought back to Earth); and a single falcon feather dropped alongside a hammer to prove they would hit the ground at the same time.

NO ONE HAS EVER WALKED ON THE MOON MORE THAN ONCE.

Moon memorials

Other objects left on the Moon are meant to remain on its surface as symbolic reminders for all time. Some are to do with peace, such as a golden olive branch and a disk with messages of goodwill from leaders of 73 countries. Others are about space travel itself, including a 8.5 cm (3 inch) "fallen astronaut" sculpture that remembers those who have died for the cause of space exploration.

Surviving the Sun?

Although footprints and objects are not swept away by water or wind, they are also not protected from the Sun by Earth's atmosphere. The US flags left behind are bleached white from the Sun now, as is the family photo left on the Moon's surface by astronaut Charles Duke.

The Fallen Astronaut sculpture in front of a memorial plaque.

Charles Duke in front of a picture of himself walking on the Moon.

FACT 32 ASTRONAUTS CAN'T BURP IN SPACE

When people are in space, gas and liquids don't separate in their stomachs as they do on Earth. You can't burp without being sick!

No upside-down burping!

When you burp, you send gas from your stomach out of your mouth. You can do this without vomiting because gases are lighter than liquids and solids, so the gas sits at the top of your stomach. If you turned upside down and tried to burp, the gas would have risen upward toward your feet and so be in the wrong place. You would vomit instead of burping.

Uh-oh, guess I better hold it in until we're back home!

Soda bubbles

In space, though, astronauts experience what we call microgravity because they are in constant free fall toward Earth. Nothing is heavier than anything else in freefall, so gases don't rise above liquids or solids. Imagine a glass of soda. The bubbles within the liquid rush toward the top of the glass and escape, right? But in microgravity, the bubbles stay inside the liquid and don't move upward. The same thing happens with gas in your stomach in space.

In space, these bubbles would never reach the top!

FACT 33

Astronauts' feet get baby soft in space because they don't walk on the ground and so the rough skin falls off.

Astronaut Sunita Williams exercising aboard the International Space Station.

Floating liquids

Liquids are always moving through our bodies. When we are on Earth, gravity helps to move these liquids downward—in microgravity this doesn't happen, so the liquids rise toward the head. NASA found that over the year that astronaut Scott Kelly spent in space, around 2,000 ml (3.5 pints) of fluid shifted into his head.

Space workouts

Space travel isn't great for your health. Your body has to work quite hard against gravity when you're on Earth just to stay upright and move around, and in microgravity astronauts' muscles quickly waste away from not being used enough as they float around. To avoid this, astronauts have to exercise for around two hours a day.

FACT 34

PEOPLE THOUGHT ASTRONAUTS MIGHT GET SPACE DISEASES

When astronauts first went into space in the 1960s, scientists were worried that they might bring back deadly new diseases and tiny alien creatures.

HORNET + 3

The Apollo 11 astronauts, meeting President Nixon while still being kept in isolation.

I'M FINE, HONEST!

Moon sickness

When the crew of Apollo 11 returned to Earth after landing on the Moon for the first time, they were not allowed back out into the world for 21 days. They stayed in a secure area undergoing a range of different tests. Scientists had no idea what diseases or alien life forms they might have accidentally brought back with them, and didn't want to risk exposing Earth to new and mysterious dangers from space.

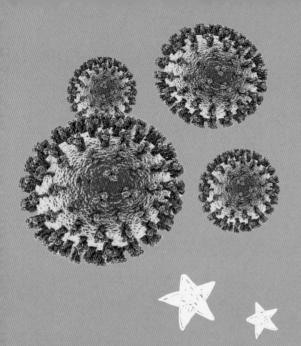

Sharing space

NASA's worries make sense—even between different countries on Earth, introducing new life forms can cause huge problems. Imagine what could happen with life from beyond Earth! When Europeans first came to the Americas, they brought diseases—such as smallpox and influenza—that killed many local people whose bodies had no resistance to them. Australia's plants and animals have also been badly affected by people bringing in species that do not naturally exist in the country.

Moon rocks

The Apollo crews also brought back quite a large amount of material from the Moon, and this could equally have carried dangerous or deadly life forms. NASA scientists kept the moon rocks in a secure space with different species of animals to make sure that they weren't poisonous or harmful in any way. They fed cockroaches moon rock and also used shrimp, oysters, and houseflies to test their safety.

A piece of rock from the Moon.

Safety first

The Apollo 12 and Apollo 14 crews (Apollo 13 wasn't able to land on the Moon) were also kept apart from others and tested in the same way when they returned to Earth. After this, scientists were convinced that there was no life on the Moon to attach itself to astronauts and pose a risk to life on Earth. People returning from space are now allowed to return home right away, after some health checks.

FACT 35

THE HUBBLE TELESCOPE SEES STARS BEING BORN

The Hubble telescope was launched in 1990 from the Discovery space shuttle. It travels around Earth taking incredible pictures of very, very far-off objects and events.

How far?

The Hubble telescope can see objects 13 billion light years away. A light year is the distance that light travels in one year—that's 9.5 trillion km (5.9 trillion miles), which is like looping around Earth 237 million times. Now multiply that by 13 billion—it's almost impossible to really imagine how far that distance really is!

Star birth as seen by Hubble

Quick, look! I think a star is being born!

THE HUBBLE TELESCOPE IS POWERED ENTIRELY BY THE SUN.

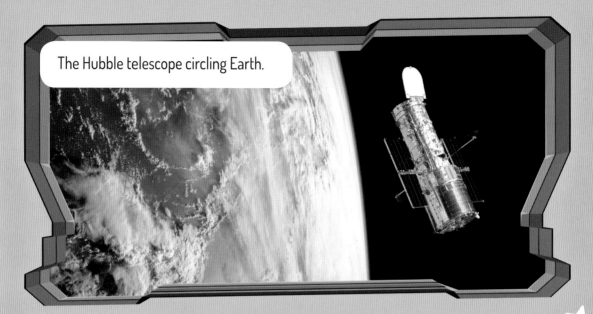

The Hubble telescope circling Earth.

Seeing clearly

Telescopes on Earth have to look through the clouds and gases of our planet's atmosphere to see out into space. This seriously limits how far they can see. In its position around 547 km (340 miles) above Earth, Hubble can see straight out into space without this hazy atmosphere getting in the way. This means it can see incredibly faint objects very far off into space.

Built for accuracy

In order to take pictures of such faint, distant objects, Hubble has to be incredibly accurate. It is built to keep very steady, which helps it to find an object and take a picture of exactly where it is. The amount to which it ever wavers its view to either side of an object is the same as about the width of a human hair seen from one mile away.

FACT **36**

The telescope is named after Edwin Hubble, who discovered that there are other galaxies beyond our own Milky Way.

Perfect mirrors

The Hubble telescope uses a system of perfectly lined-up mirrors to see deep into space. These mirrors are incredibly precisely made to ensure that they can see things as accurately as possible. Hubble's main mirror is so finely polished that if you scaled it up to be as wide as the Earth there wouldn't be any bumps more than around 15 cm (6 inches) tall.

Edwin Hubble was a talented athlete and basketball coach, as well as a famous astronomer.

45

THE FIRST ANIMALS IN SPACE WERE FRUIT FLIES

Two fruit flies were launched into space in a rocket in 1947. The rocket just passed over the Karman Line 100 km (60 miles) up from Earth's surface, which is considered the start of space.

This is one small flight for flies, one giant leap for flykind!

There's no fruit in space, what are we going to eat?!

Flying high

As humans, we think pretty highly of ourselves compared with other animals. But despite all our cleverness, the humble fruit fly beat us into space! Scientists wanted to check how safe space travel was for humans, so they sent up two fruit flies in a rocket to see what happened to them. Luckily for the flies, they came safely back down to Earth and survived to buzz another day!

FACT 38

A number of animals have been bred in space, including jellyfish, frogs, and sea urchins.

Why fruit flies?

You wouldn't think that humans and fruit flies have a lot in common, but actually we're more similar than we look! Our genes contain information about our bodies and what they do, and over 60% of disease-causing genes in humans have recognizable matches in fruit flies. This means that looking at how fruit flies were affected by space travel could tell us quite a lot about what might happen to humans.

Weightless apes

Before humans went up into space, scientists were very concerned that we may not survive long periods of weightlessness. We share about 99% of our genetic code—our DNA—with chimpanzees, so in 1961 US scientists launched a chimpanzee named Ham into space to see how it affected him. He returned safe and well, just a little tired and thirsty. This mission paved the way for the successful first human astronaut launch later that year.

IN 1973, A SPIDER SPAN THE FIRST EVER WEB IN SPACE.

Animal heroes

Many other animals have been launched into space, including dogs, mice, rats, rabbits, insects, tortoises, fish, frogs, jellyfish, snails, and spiders. Sadly some of these animals did not survive, and we owe them a huge amount in helping us understand how to make space travel safe for humans. Scientists have continued to test how space affects animals in different ways and what long-term effects space travel might have on humans.

Ham, the chimpanzee astronaut.

A Russian stamp dedicated to Laika, the first dog in space.

47

THERE ARE AROUND 70 BILLION TRILLION STARS

If you counted up every single grain of sand in all the deserts and beaches on Earth, it would still be less than the number of stars in the known universe.

Stars and galaxies

In our galaxy, the Milky Way, there are more than 300 billion stars—that's 40 times as many as there are people on Earth. Scientists believe there are around 100 billion galaxies in the known universe. Some are much smaller than ours, but the total number of stars in the universe is so big it's hard to really imagine it.

I thought us stars were special?

Sorry pal, we're pretty common!

Using a basic telescope on a clear, dark night, you could see up to 2.65 million stars.

Seeing stars

Around 9,000 stars are bright enough for someone with average vision to see at night without a telescope or binoculars, but you can't see more than half the sky at any one time. This means that on a clear, dark night you could see an absolute maximum of around 4,500 stars. In most places the number will be much lower, though, as nearby night-time light—for example, from buildings and street lamps—drowns out the fainter stars.

A satellite image of light pollution at night.

Measuring brightness

The brightness of stars and planets is measured on a magnitude scale. The bigger the magnitude, the fainter the star is. On Earth the faintest stars we can see with the naked eye are magnitude +6.5, but with a small pair of binoculars you can see stars at magnitude +9. There are far more faint stars than bright ones, so using binoculars like this reveals up to around 108,000 stars across your half of the sky.

Galaxy gazing

Because Earth is at the end of one of our galaxy's four "arms," we can actually see the Milky Way in the sky. Except that most of us can't any more ... today, two-thirds of the world live in towns and cities that are too bright for people to see the Milky Way. Many countries now have International Dark Reserves, areas kept free from light pollution, to make sure we don't lose our views of space for ever.

The Alqueva Dark Sky Reserve in Portugal

FACT
41

Dung beetles can use the Milky Way to navigate.

NEUTRON STARS CAN SPIN 700 TIMES A SECOND

A neutron star is the tiny, dense core of a star that has collapsed in on itself. Just as an ice skater spins faster when they pull in their arms, so a star speeds up as it shrinks.

Packed in

Becoming a neutron star is one of the possible ways that a star's life can end. Neutron stars are incredibly dense, which means that they have a huge amount of matter crammed into a very small area. A neutron star packs around 1.4 times the mass of our Sun into a ball around the width of a small city.

Woah! That's a lot of spin!

Most of an atom is empty space.

No space

You are mostly made of empty space, and so is everything around you. This is because everything is made of atoms and over 99.9% of an atom is empty space. If you could remove all empty space inside the human body, every person on Earth could be squished inside an area the size of a sugar cube. A neutron star has had all its empty space crushed out of it, so only matter remains.

A pulsar.

Pulsars

There are different types of neutron stars, including strongly magnetic magnetars and extra-fast-spinning pulsars. From Earth, a pulsar looks like a star flashing on and off—it gives out two steady beams of light, but as it spins the beams go in and out of view. Jocelyn Bell Burnell first discovered pulsars in 1967, and the team of scientists studying them first thought they might be attempts by aliens to talk to us— they even named the first pulsar "Little Green Men 1!"

Star finales

A star only ends its life by exploding and turning into a neutron star if it is a certain size—too small and it becomes a white dwarf, too big and it collapses entirely into a black hole. Our Sun will become a white dwarf—when it runs out of fuel to burn, it will lose its outer layers and its hot core will slowly cool over a billion years or so.

It doesn't look little or green to me!

FACT 43

YOU CAN SEE INTO THE PAST

When you look at stars, you are seeing into their past. Because of how long light from stars takes to reach us, they may not even exist any more by the time we can see them.

Long-distance travel

Light travels incredibly quickly, almost 300,000 km (186,000 miles) in a single second. But many stars are so far away from Earth that it can still take a very, very long time for light to travel from where a star is to where we are.

Our photos of this spiral galaxy, M81, show it as it looked 12 million years ago.

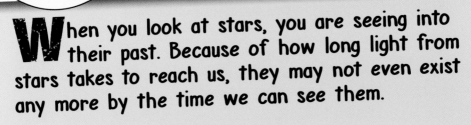

I can't believe what I'm seeing!

FACT 44

If you moved at the speed of light, you could travel around Earth seven times in a single second.

Sun light

The Sun is by far the closest star to Earth, but light doesn't travel to us from the Sun in an instant—the journey takes around eight minutes. You must NEVER look at the Sun directly, because it can seriously damage your eyes and even leave you blind, but if you could you would be seeing the Sun as it looked eight minutes ago rather than right now.

Seeing the past

Other stars and planets are a lot, lot farther away than the Sun and so we are seeing much farther into their past. Scientists using powerful telescopes can see stars so far away that the light from them has taken billions of years to reach us. In this time, a star may have run out of fuel and ended its life—but we won't see this change for billions of years.

Dinosaurs on Earth

If there are aliens somewhere in the universe that are capable of seeing far into space, they will see Earth as it looked in the past—how far in the past depends on how far away they are from us. If they are far enough away that light from Earth takes 65 million years to reach them, they would see our planet as it looked in the time of the dinosaurs.

FACT 45 STARS ARE BORN IN GIANT GAS CLOUDS

A nebula is a huge cloud of dust and gases floating in space. Some of this dust and gas squashes together and heats up until lots of energy is created. The star is born and shines brightly.

Pulling together

So what makes a cloud of gas form itself into a star? Well, at first, gravity—the same force that pulls you down to Earth's surface. Gas particles are very weakly attracted to each other because of gravity, and as they come together the force of gravity then keeps pulling in more and more gas.

FACT 46 Horseshoe, Crab, Cat's Eye, Boomerang, Bubble, Ant, Tarantula, and Stingray are all real names of nebulae.

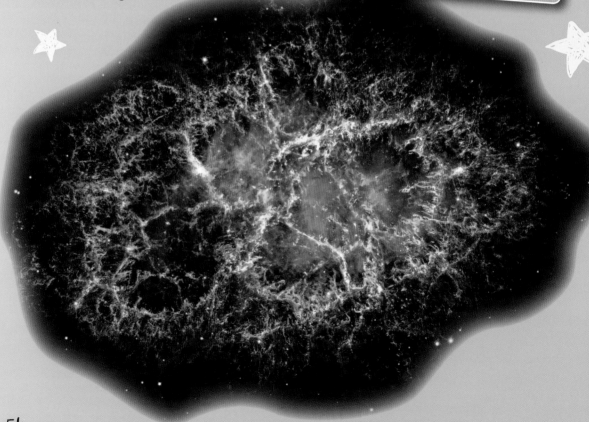

Under pressure

As the gas cloud grows, the gravity squeezes it together and it gets hotter and higher-pressured. Eventually the pressure forces the cloud to start collapsing in toward its middle and it becomes a protostar. A protostar looks like a star but it is still forming, so it keeps pulling in gas and getting hotter and denser. This stage can last between 100,000 and 10 million years, depending how big a star is being formed.

Star birth

When a protostar's core is hot and pressured enough, the materials there change and give out a huge amount of energy. A star is born! It has begun burning its limited supply of fuel—when the fuel runs out the star will die, but it has billions of years before that happens.

Failed stars

If a protostar doesn't manage to reach a big enough mass as it is forming, its core can't get hot enough to jump-start the reaction that turns it into a star. Instead, it settles into its new state as a brown dwarf. Brown dwarves are something between a giant gassy planet, such as Jupiter, and a small star. They create some light, like a star—but they have atmosphere with clouds and even storms, like a planet.

FACT 47
THE SUN IS A PRETTY AVERAGE STAR

The Sun is literally everything to us on Earth—we couldn't exist without it—but it's nothing special in the star world. There are stars a fraction of its size and others more than a thousand times larger.

The biggest

The Sun is huge in comparison to Earth, but not compared to other stars. The largest star that scientists are aware of today is UY Scuti, a red hypergiant that is more than 1,700 times the size of the Sun. If we could drop UY Scuti into our solar system in the Sun's place, it would swallow up everything out as far as Saturn.

FACT 48

Most stars that can be seen with the naked eye are bigger than the Sun.

Yeah well, everyone knows the best things come in small packages.

But wait ...

UY Scuti may take up the most space, but it has a much smaller mass than other stars. Interestingly, stars' sizes and masses do not always match up as you'd imagine—especially when it comes to giant stars. The star R136a1 is only around 30 times the size of the Sun but has 265 times its mass. UY Scuti is lightweight in comparison, with only 30 times the Sun's mass.

The smallest

The smallest star ever discovered is EBLM J0555-57Ab, and scientists think it is as small as a star can be. If a star doesn't get to a high enough mass as it is forming, it will become a brown dwarf rather than a star. EBLM J0555-57Ab is only a touch bigger than Saturn, which fits into the Sun around 1600 times over. It is a very faint star, around 2,000–3,000 times fainter than the Sun.

FACT 49

The closest stars to our Sun are over four light years away. They are a set of three stars called Alpha Centauri.

Alpha Centauri has two main stars and a third, fainter one tagging along too.

Lone star

The Sun does stand out from other stars in one way—it hasn't got any friends. Most stars have a companion star not too far away, and some are part of a system of three or four stars. Nearly all stars form with a companion, so scientists think the Sun might have lost its one at some point.

FACT 50
STARS HAVE STARQUAKES LIKE OUR EARTHQUAKES

Have you ever felt an earthquake? The ground shakes as the plates making up the Earth's outer layer shift around. Something similar happens on certain stars, but it's more powerful than an earthquake.

Mysterious magnetars

Starquakes take place on magnetars—small, very dense, strongly magnetic stars. A magnetar is a mysterious type of star—scientists have only ever identified 23 of them. It has by far the strongest magnetic field of any object in the universe, and scientists think it is the core that remains after a supermassive star dies.

FACT 51

A starquake sent out the brightest flash scientists have ever seen from beyond our solar system.

Earthquakes can cause huge damage as they tear through the Earth's crust.

Ain't nobody stronger than me!

Core and crust

Magnetars are so dense that scientists think at their centre there may be a hot, soupy core in which materials have been crushed into incredibly small particles. Around this core there is probably a thick, incredibly hot iron crystal crust that makes up most of the star's volume. The material deep inside this crust is called "nuclear pasta," and scientists think it is the strongest material in the known universe.

Bursting out

Scientists think that a starquake happens when a magnetar's magnetic field moves with so much force it rips through its crust. Apparently, the strongest material in the universe is no match for the incredible power of a starquake! The movement of the magnetic field also pulls the star's core like an elastic band, which eventually snaps—a fireball of particles and radiation shoots out of the rip in the crust.

FACT
52
Scientists have only ever recorded three starquakes—in 1979, 1998, and 2004.

A starquake in action

High energy

A starquake gives out a giant blast of energy so violent that one can affect us on Earth when it happens on a star 50,000 light years away. In 2004, a burst of energy from a starquake disrupted radio and submarine signals, took satellites offline, and actually moved the Earth's magnetic field. Luckily, it only lasted for a tenth of a second!

FACT 53 A BLACK HOLE CAN TEAR APART A STAR

In 2018, for the first time ever, scientists were able to watch an enormous black hole grab a star with its powerful gravity and shred it apart.

Black holes

A black hole forms when a large star dies and collapses in on itself. It has a huge mass in a small space, and its gravity is incredibly strong. In fact, a black hole's pull of gravity is so great that it creates a one-way system into itself—it draws in objects and light, which can then never escape.

FACT 54

There is a black hole, named Sagittarius A, in the middle of our galaxy.

Yikes!

Mwahahahaha, you can't get away!

Finding proof

Scientists have believed for a while that black holes are capable of destroying stars caught at their edge. They worked out that this would create an enormous blast and send a jet of matter shooting out across space at great speed. In 2018, they actually saw the jet, confirming their theory.

Seeing the invisible

Because no light can get out of them, black holes are invisible to us. Scientists use powerful telescopes and special equipment to find them in space. They look at how stars and other matter in an area of space move—when there is a black hole they spin around it and create a flat disk. The spinning matter gives off different types of radiation that scientists can record.

Don't panic!

A black hole sounds terrifying—invisible, destructive, with enough power to tear apart a star. But it doesn't zoom around the universe looking for its next kill and although it has very strong pulling power it can't suck in stars and planets from anywhere in space. A black hole can only destroy a star that passes very close to its edge.

FACT
55

Until 1967, black holes did not have one set name—scientists called them different things, including "collapsar" and "frozen star."

I'm panicking!

FACT 56
YOU ARE MADE OF STAR DUST

Most of the basic materials that make up our bodies were formed in stars over billions of years and journeyed across the universe when stars exploded.

That's where we come from.

Human elements

An element is a material that cannot be broken down into any simpler substance. The human body is mostly made up of four elements, which are oxygen, carbon, hydrogen, and nitrogen. We also contain smaller amounts of many other elements, including calcium, sodium, chlorine, copper, tin, iron, and zinc.

The stuff of stars

Scientists can work out what a star is made of by looking at the light that it gives out. Every element within a star gives out light of a different wavelength, so by measuring the bright and dark patches of a star's light scientists can work out which elements it contains. Scientists have found that humans and stars share almost all of the same elements, although not in the same amounts.

Zinc is one of the elements that makes up both our galaxy and our body.

Multiple lifetimes

When certain stars approach the end of their life, they push out most of their mass in a huge explosion called a supernova. This matter is then recycled to create new stars, which eventually go supernova too and continue this cycle.

The Big Bang

Scientists think it is also possible that some of the hydrogen in our bodies actually came from the Big Bang—the huge explosion that created the universe. In the early days of the universe only the very lightest elements, hydrogen and helium, existed—they still make up 98% of the universe today. Over time, stars created other, heavier elements by squeezing atoms together in their hot, high-pressure cores.

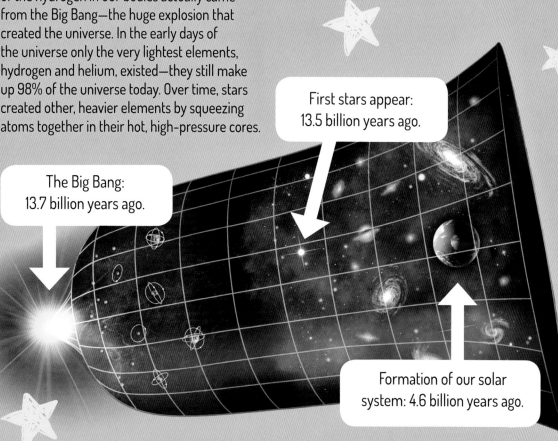

First stars appear:
13.5 billion years ago.

The Big Bang:
13.7 billion years ago.

Formation of our solar system: 4.6 billion years ago.

THE UNIVERSE ISN'T MAKING MANY NEW STARS

Scientists believe that half of all the stars that have ever existed were created between 9 and 11 billion years ago. The rate of new stars being born has fallen hugely since then.

Slacking off

An international team of scientists found in 2012 that since the universe's star-making peak 11 billion years ago it has really been slacking off. The star birth rate has dropped by 97% from that peak to its current slump today. If this same trend continues, it will mean that 95% of all stars that will ever exist in the universe have been born already.

The Pillars of Creation is an area of space that has birthed many new stars, but it may be well past its peak now.

Hi-tech study

The team of scientists who made this discovery used three advanced telescopes to collect around ten times as much information as any previous similar study. They looked at a range of star-making galaxies at different distances from Earth, and were able to work out how quickly stars were forming at various points in the universe's history by measuring the light from clouds of gas and dust in these galaxies.

The Subaru telescope in Hawaii was used to discover the falling star birth rate.

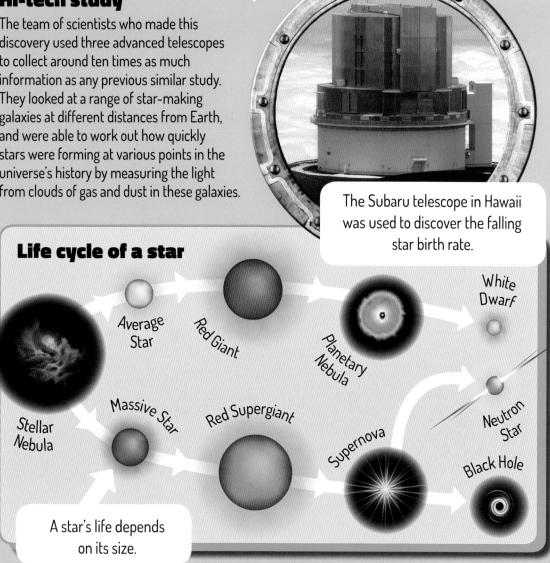

Life cycle of a star

Stellar Nebula

Average Star

Red Giant

Planetary Nebula

White Dwarf

Massive Star

Red Supergiant

Supernova

Neutron Star

Black Hole

A star's life depends on its size.

Healthy galaxy

Many of the universe's billions of galaxies may no longer be forming stars, but our galaxy—the Milky Way—is in pretty good shape. Lucky us! As one of the universe's healthy, star-birthing galaxies, the Milky Way will play an important part in the universe's future.

Why so slow?

We are not sure why the star birth rate has slowed so much over time, but a 2017 study suggests that magnetic fields might be to blame. Scientists created a computer simulation of a particular galaxy—using all the known information about it to make their model as accurate as possible—and found that magnetic forces in the middle of the galaxy stopped its clouds of dust and gas from collapsing and forming stars.

EXPLODING STARS CAN OUTSHINE ENTIRE GALAXIES

When a star explodes at the end of its life, it is called a supernova. A supernova gives out a huge amount of light, which can sometimes be seen from Earth.

FACT 59

Scientists recently discovered a star lost in the glare of a supernova for 21 years.

A-maz-ing!

Supernova spotting

Around 1,800 years ago, scientists in China spotted a very bright star that didn't move, as they knew comets do, and that took around eight months to fade. This seems to be the first record of anyone seeing a supernova. The last sighting was a while ago now—back in 1604, when William Shakespeare was alive! This supernova is named after Johannes Kepler, a scientist who spotted it but mistook it for a new type of star.

Wow, kind of puts the Sun to shame ...

One every second

There is a supernova somewhere in the known universe roughly once every second. Count to ten slowly ... that's ten stars that have exploded in a violent blaze of light! There should be a supernova in our galaxy, the Milky Way, every 50 years or so—but they are tricky to spot. There was one visible from Earth 100 years ago but from historical records of the time it doesn't seem like anyone saw it at all.

FACT 60

A supernova can give out more light than our Sun does in its entire lifetime.

Supernova pretenders

Sometimes stars undergo explosions but aren't actually destroyed by them, as they would be in a supernova. During this type of event, a star gives out a huge amount of energy and becomes much brighter for a short time, before returning to its previous state. The huge amount of light given out is easily mistaken for a supernova.

Watch a star explode

There is due to be a supernova in 2022 that should be visible from Earth with the naked eye. This is the first supernova that scientists have said will happen within a set time period—in the past, they haven't been so confident of knowing exactly when one will take place. When the star system explodes it will become more than 10,000 times brighter, and stay bright for most of the next year.

FACT 61 SOME PLANETS HAVE TWO SUNS

More than half of all star systems in the known universe circle around two stars rather than one. Can you imagine having a second sun in the sky?

Strange as fiction

Our solar system has one Sun, but more than half of all solar systems in the known universe circle around two stars. Planets that circle around two stars are officially called "circumbinary planets" but sometimes they are also known as "Tatooine planets"—after Luke Skywalker's home planet in *Star Wars*, which famously has two suns.

FACT 62

Scientists have found planets with three suns and one giant planet with four suns.

Two suns? At least I remembered enough sunglasses!

Changing journeys

We move regularly around the Sun—one journey all the way around takes 365 (and ¼) days, an Earth year. (We have a Leap Year every four years to make up the quarter-days.) But for planets with more than one sun, it isn't so simple. Their movement is much more irregular and their journey time—and sometimes even their path—around their suns varies.

Hard to find

The Kepler space observatory, which looks for Earth-size planets orbiting other stars, has found a number of planets with two suns. But it's not easy—because of their irregular movement, scientists find it quite tricky to spot these planets. They search for small dips in a star's brightness, as these suggest that a planet could be passing in front of it and blocking a little bit of its light.

Right, I'm lost. Which star was it next?

In the Kepler-47 system, two planets move around two suns.

Rare planets

Although most star systems have more than one star, it is quite rare for a two-star system to have any planets moving around it. The Kepler space observatory has found 2,600 planets beyond our solar system, but only 11 of them circle around more than one star. Scientists think that the magnetic force of the stars may hurl planets away from them, out of orbit.

The Kepler telescope was launched into space aboard a rocket in 2009.

69

FLYING THROUGH THE ASTEROID BELT IS EASY

Movies and TV shows often show spacecraft struggling to fly through areas with lots of asteroids, dodging between huge speeding rocks. The reality is much less exciting.

Asteroid belt

Asteroids are rocky objects, leftover bits and pieces from when the solar system formed billions of years ago, which still circle around the Sun. In our solar system, between the planets Mars and Jupiter, there is an area of space containing millions of asteroids. This is known as the asteroid belt, and most of the asteroids in our solar system are found within it.

Saturn

Jupiter

Asteroid belt

Mars

Earth

What?!
I was expecting
a challenge!

Venus

Space between

Although there are lots of asteroids to avoid, there is typically around 1 to 2.9 million km (620,000 to 1.8 million miles) between each one. It's difficult to even get close enough to an asteroid to see it as you're flying through the belt, let alone having to constantly dodge around them! You really have to aim at a particular asteroid in order to be sure of seeing one.

This is a disappointingly boring flight.

Not all alike

The largest known asteroid, Vesta, is 578 km (359 miles) wide, although most are much smaller than this. Asteroids are made of rock and metal, and the different types and amounts of the materials that make them up change how they look. For example, asteroids that contain lots of metal are shiny.

Beyond the belt

Although most of the asteroids in our solar system are found in the asteroid belt, there are some in other areas too. For instance, Trojans are what we call asteroids that circle around Jupiter. A number of asteroids pass close to Earth, and are known (a bit unimaginatively) as Near-Earth Asteroids—the ones that might be dangerous for Earth are the "Earth-crossers," asteroids that actually cross Earth's path and so could crash into us!

COMETS ARE DIRTY SPACE SNOWBALLS

A comet is made of a mixture of frozen gases and water ice with bits of rock and dust stuck in it. These materials come from the time when our solar system was formed.

Gas tail

Dust tail

Icy core

Who are you calling a dirty space snowball?

Two tails

Comets are made up of an icy core and a trailing tail. In fact, most comets have one blue tail made of gas and another brighter tail made of dust. It is the Sun's light hitting the dust particles in this tail that makes it shine so brightly. As the comet moves closer to the Sun, the sunlight pushes these dust particles back away into a long tail that can stretch for almost 10 million km (6 million miles).

Mercury

Earth

Venus

Mars

Asteroid Belt

Jupiter

Saturn

Uranus

Neptune

Kuiper Belt

Oort Cloud

The Kuiper Belt

Comets in our solar system come from one of two places—the nearest one to us is the Kuiper Belt. This is a huge, disk-shaped area that begins close to Neptune and continues past Pluto, containing many different icy objects. The comets that come from the Kuiper Belt are short-period comets, which take less than 200 years to circle around the Sun.

The Oort Cloud

The Oort Cloud is around 100 times farther away than the Kuiper Belt, running all around the edge of our solar system like a giant shell. No one knows for sure how many objects there are in the Oort Cloud, but it may be around 2 trillion—around 266 times as many people on Earth. Scientists think that long-period comets, which take longer than 200 years to circle around the Sun, come from this area.

A photo of Halley's Comet, taken in 1910.

Star finales

The most famous comet (for people on our planet, at least!) is Halley's Comet. It takes around 75 years to circle all the way around the Sun, and we can only see it at one certain point in this journey. Seeing the comet is a once-in-a-lifetime event for all but the very luckiest people. It was last visible from Earth in 1986 and may be able to be seen again in 2061. Don't miss it!

I've been waiting for years to see this comet!

73

A HUGE CLOUD OF WATER FLOATS THROUGH SPACE

Scientists have found a cloud far off in outer space that holds 140 trillion times the water in the Earth's oceans. It is the biggest amount of water that we have identified.

How much?

140 trillion is such a huge number that it's hard to even imagine how big it really is. Think about it this way—if you counted out 140 trillion seconds, it would take more than 4 million years! Our galaxy, the Milky Way, has a few large clouds of water, but this giant is around 4,000 times bigger than any of them.

I feel so small ...

Most of the water in our galaxy is in the form of ice.

Old water

Scientists believe that this area of water is around 12 billion years old—to give an idea of just how old that really is, the universe only came into existence around 13.8 billion years ago. This means that water was one of the first materials ever created. Before the cloud's discovery, scientists thought that water was first created around a billion years after we now know it was.

Finding the cloud

This cloud is so far away from Earth that it has taken light from where it is in space around 12 billion years to reach us. Light travels faster than anything else in the known universe, so that's a pretty long way away! Amazingly, we have developed such powerful telescopes that scientists were able to discover the cloud using two of them in Hawaii and California.

Black hole

As if being a universe-wide record breaker for holding water wasn't dramatic enough, this giant cloud also surrounds a huge black hole! This black hole has 20 billion times the mass of the Sun and it is part of a strange, giant object called a quasar that gives out a huge amount of energy.

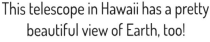

This telescope in Hawaii has a pretty beautiful view of Earth, too!

ASTEROIDS CAN HAVE THEIR OWN MOONS

Some of the bigger asteroids in our solar system have moons of their own. In 1993, a tiny moon was spotted for the first time circling the asteroid 243 Ida.

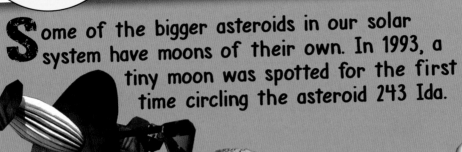

> Hi, Galileo, I'm 243 Ida and this is my moon, Dactyl!

Dactyl

The name of 243 Ida's moon is Dactyl. It is only 1.6 km (1 mile) across, almost 20 times smaller than the asteroid. Dactyl moves quite slowly, circling 243 Ida at around 36 km (22 miles) per hour, which is only a bit faster than a person sprinting. Although Dactyl is pretty small and slow, it's still an impressive record-breaker—the first moon of an asteroid ever discovered and photographed.

Galileo spacecraft

Dactyl was discovered by the Galileo space mission in 1993. The Galileo spacecraft was launched—with no one aboard—in 1989. It was the first spacecraft to explore Jupiter and its moons for a long period of time, circling around Jupiter for eight years. It took many pictures and measurements, teaching us more about this huge planet and its moons, but it also studied and photographed asteroids.

Scientists think that Jupiter has at least 79 moons!

Not so special

Since this first sighting of an asteroid with a moon circling around it, scientists have discovered several more asteroids in our solar system that also have moons. In total, we know of more than 200 asteroids—both within and beyond our solar system—that have moons. In fact, there are asteroids that have more than one moon. A huge asteroid called 3122 Florence, which came pretty close to Earth in 2017, has two moons.

Dwarf planets

We know that some planets have moons, and that asteroids can too, but what about another player in our solar system—dwarf planets? Well, Pluto may have been downgraded from a planet to a dwarf planet in 2006, but of the dwarf planets it is both the biggest and has the most moons—five! Haumea has two, Eris and Makemake each have one, and Ceres—which lies in the asteroid belt between Mars and Jupiter—doesn't have a moon.

PLUTO, 5 moons

HAUMEA, 2 moons

MAKEMAKE, 1 moon

ERIS, 1 moon

CERES, 0 moons

FACT 68
EARTH DESTROYS A CAR-SIZED ASTEROID EVERY YEAR

About once a year, an asteroid the size of a car hits Earth's atmosphere—the mix of gases that surround our planet. This creates an impressive fireball, which burns up before reaching Earth's surface.

50 rhinos a day

Every day, more than 100 tons of material—roughly the combined weight of 50 rhinos—falls from space toward us. Although this is a lot of material, the individual pieces aren't normally very big. In fact, it is largely space dust and objects smaller than a grain of sand. Most of it burns up as it enters Earth's atmosphere, the layers of gases around our planet.

Wheeeee!

FACT
69

Asteroids aren't that big, in space terms. If you rolled together all the asteroids known in our solar system, they would only make up 4% of the Moon.

Burning up

When objects travel through space, they can reach very high speeds. When they hit the Earth's atmosphere at this speed, they squash the gas particles in the atmosphere in front of them as they go. A gas that gets squashed like this gets hotter. This makes the object heat up too, until it gets so hot that it burns up.

Shuttle safety

When spacecraft return to Earth from space, they obviously have to re-enter our planet's atmosphere. So why don't they burn up like the other objects falling to Earth from space? Well, if we're not very careful, they do. Obviously we don't want that—especially if there are people on board. Spacecraft either have special insulating tiles to stop them getting too hot or they have a heat shield designed to melt away and carry off the heat.

A space capsule re-entering Earth's atmosphere, its heat shield glowing red-hot.

Danger from beyond

Some objects are big enough that they burn up a bit when they hit Earth's atmosphere but not entirely. Usually the remains that hit the Earth are very small and don't cause a problem. But if an asteroid more than 1 km (0.62 miles) across hit Earth's atmosphere, it could have a global impact. There are asteroids in our solar system big enough to wipe out life on Earth, but they are too far away to be a danger.

An asteroid? Yikes!

SHOOTING STARS ARE NOT STARS AT ALL

Meteors are often called "shooting stars" because they look like bright stars moving across the sky, but they are not stars at all.

Not a star

A star appears as a still point of light in the night sky, and a meteor appears as a fast-moving streak of light. But although a meteor looks like a speeding star, they are actually very different. A star is a huge ball of burning gas far off in space, whereas a meteor is the glowing path of a small piece of rock or other matter that has entered Earth's atmosphere—the layers of gases that surround our planet—from space.

It's so beautiful ...

Yeah, not bad for a load of rocks and gas balls.

Burning bright

This small piece of rock or other matter from space, usually between the size of a grain of sand and a boulder, is called a meteoroid. When it hits Earth's atmosphere, it gets so hot that it burns up and changes into a gas. This burning gives off light, like a fire does, and we can see its visible path across the sky as a bright, glowing streak—which we call a meteor.

Meteoroids, meteors, meteorites?

So now we know that a meteoroid is an object and a meteor is the light that it gives off as it burns up, let's look at meteorites ... Basically, if any part of an object from space makes it down to Earth's surface without burning up entirely in its atmosphere, it's a meteorite! It can be the leftover part of a meteoroid, an asteroid (which is bigger) or a comet (which is icy).

Meteorites found on Earth

FACT 71

Meteor showers that are especially intense are called meteor storms. During these events, you could see more than 1,000 meteors in an hour!

Meteor showers

If you've ever been lucky enough to see a meteor, you'll know how special it feels to watch it zipping across the sky. Now imagine if you could see 100 of them in an hour! Meteor showers happen when lots of small objects fall into Earth's atmosphere at once, meaning that for a certain length of time—usually several days—there are lots more meteors to spot than normal.

FACT 72
SCIENTISTS LANDED A SPACECRAFT ON A COMET

In 2016, for the very first time ever, a team of scientists managed to successfully land on the surface of a speeding comet. That's some careful driving!

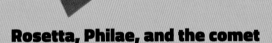

Can't you stay still for a second?! This is really hard!

Rosetta, Philae, and the comet

The lander that actually touched down on the comet was called Philae, and it was part of Rosetta, a larger spacecraft that had been following the comet for around two years. Rosetta launched in 2004 but took 10 years to arrive at its target comet. This comet, called 67P/Churyumov–Gerasimenko, is named after the two scientists who first discovered it in 1969.

FACT 73
Earth was often hit by comets early in its life, and scientists believe they may have given us some of the water for our oceans.

Moving target

67P/Churyumov–Gerasimenko is around 4 km (2.5 miles) across, which sounds quite big but as it travels at up to 135,000 km (84,000 miles) an hour it's not an easy target on which to land. Imagine it by thinking of trying to land on an area the length of Central Park in New York, while Central Park is moving at more than 300 times the speed of the fastest car in the world.

Bumpy landing

As Philae dropped down toward the comet, it took close-up photographs to help scientists understand more about comets. Unfortunately, Philae's landing wasn't a smooth one—it bounced twice and ended up in a shadowy area, where its solar batteries couldn't get enough light to charge up properly. In July 2015, as the comet passed nearby the Sun, it woke up again but soon ran out of power once more.

Philae landing craft.

Mission end

The Philae lander is still attached to the comet, and scientists hope that it may still send back more photos in future. For the Rosetta spacecraft, however, the end came in September 2016 when it crash landed into the comet. This was a planned end to the mission, as the comet is heading out into the outer reaches of our solar system. There isn't enough sunlight out there to continue powering Rosetta to fly through space with it.

That comet can't hurt me now!

FACT
74

In 1910, Earth passed through the tail of a comet. Some people were so scared about its possible effects, that they bought "anti-comet" umbrellas!

HUMANS ARE LEAVING JUNK IN SPACE

There are more than 17,000 man-made objects circling around Earth—and these are only the ones large enough to be tracked.

Bits and pieces

We think there are around 170 million smaller pieces of space junk, too, from paint flakes to nuts and bolts. Even the very tiniest objects can damage spacecraft. Bigger objects can be very dangerous if spacecraft crash into them because they are moving so fast—faster than a speeding bullet— as they circle around the Earth.

Come on guys, clean up after yourselves!

No longer needed

There are more than 1,400 working satellites circling around Earth, but there are also lots of old satellites that aren't in use any more. There are many pieces of burned-out equipment used to launch missions into space, left behind over 60 years of exploring space. There is a risk of this space junk crashing into working satellites and damaging them.

One of the many satellites circling Earth.

Chain reaction

Every time pieces of space junk crash into each other, more bits can break off and increase the total number of unwanted objects floating around Earth. If objects have any leftover fuel or batteries, they may also explode and send out lots of smaller bits. The only way to control the amount of junk circling around Earth is to remove the larger items.

Clearing up

RemoveDebris is a small, experimental satellite sent out into space to try out clearing up some of this space junk. In 2018 it caught its first piece in a test run—it sent out a target, which it then recaptured in a net, and the satellite and space junk fell back to Earth to burn up in the atmosphere. A net seems like a strangely simple idea, but it seems to do the job!

Space junk crashing into the International Space Station could be very dangerous for the astonauts on board.

85

FACT 76
MOST METEORITES ARE SMALLER THAN AN ORANGE

Every day, tons of meteorites reach the Earth's surface. But don't worry too much about getting hit by one on its way down—each one is usually tiny, no more than a speck of dust!

What is a meteorite?

A meteorite is an object that has come from space and crossed through Earth's atmosphere, the layers of gases that surround our planet, before landing somewhere on its surface. It was originally part of a larger (but still relatively small) object, which burned up as it hit Earth's atmosphere until only this small bit remained. This larger object may itself be a broken-off piece of an asteroid or a comet.

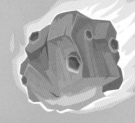

The orange looks tastier!

FACT 77
Meteorites have been spotted on the surface of Mars and other planets.

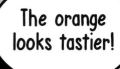

A meteorite falling into the ocean.

Where do they land?

Over 70% of the Earth's surface is covered in water, so it makes sense that most meteorites end up landing in the water rather than on land. They fall randomly all over the world, but it is easiest to spot and collect the ones that have landed in desert areas—both hot, sandy deserts and cold, snowy areas such as Antarctica.

Crashes and craters

If a meteorite is big enough, it creates a visible crater when it crash-lands. A crater is a bowl-shaped dip in the ground, with a raised ring around its top edge. There are fewer than 200 impact craters on Earth, but the Moon has thousands all over its surface. Earth's atmosphere slows down and burns up falling objects, but the Moon gets the full impact of any crash landing.

FACT 78

Dust in your home contains tiny burned bits of meteorite.

Not just meteorites

Asteroids and comets can also crash-land on our planet's surface. Like meteorites, they will partly burn up as they pass through Earth's atmosphere, but what survives and hits Earth can be much bigger than any meteorite. This means that they can create much bigger craters, and even have a worldwide impact—scientists believe an asteroid hitting Earth led to the dinosaurs dying out.

This impact crater was made almost 50,000 years ago.

FACT 79

TOYS ARE FLYING THROUGH SPACE RIGHT NOW

When NASA launched the Juno spacecraft in 2011, there were three special guests on board ... They are circling around Jupiter, farther away from Earth than any human has ever been.

Wow, this sure beats the view from inside our toy chest ...

Hi-tech toys

These space explorers aren't your average toys. They are LEGO® figures made entirely from a special type of space-grade metal that has been tested to make sure it won't interfere with anything on board. The trio are models of the ancient Roman god Jupiter, his wife Juno, and the scientist Galileo Galilei—who discovered the four largest moons of planet Jupiter.

Juno and Jupiter

The Juno spacecraft is on a mission to explore Jupiter and bring back more information about the largest planet in our solar system. It is hoped that this new knowledge should help scientists further develop ideas about the creation of giant planets and of our solar system. The onboard crew of three also have a further mission—to get more children interested in space travel.

Galileo Galilei

Ancient Romans thought Jupiter and Juno ruled over the other gods and goddesses.

The planet Jupiter and the Juno spacecraft circling around it.

Toys in space

These three special passengers aren't the first toys to go into space—several toys have been flown up to the International Space Station. Buzz Lightyear, from the movie *Toy Story*, has also spent 450 days in space, including a year aboard the International Space Station.

Along for the ride

As well as toys, there have been a number of interesting objects launched into space over the years. In 2018, billionaire Elon Musk launched a sports car into space aboard a rocket, and it is still speeding through our solar system.

FACT 80

A DAY IS LONGER THAN A YEAR ON VENUS

A day is how long a planet takes to spin all the way around. A year is how long it takes to circle the Sun. A Venus day is 243 Earth days— a year is only 225.

Slow spinner

Venus spins round veeeerry slowly compared with the other planets in our solar system, including Earth. This is why its days are so long. Weirdly, it doesn't always spin around at the same speed. Although it takes around 243 Earth days for Venus to turn all the way around and complete a day, the exact time can vary by up to seven minutes. Scientists are still not entirely sure why.

NEW DAY

LOADING ...

Odd one out

Venus also turns in the opposite direction of Earth and most other planets. And although its solid body takes 243 Earth days to turn all the way around, its atmosphere—the layers of gases around it—takes only four Earth days to complete the same rotation. Imagine the sky and the clouds on Earth spinning round 60 times faster than the planet under your feet—it's enough to make you dizzy!

Different days

Venus has the longest day of any planet in our solar system. A day on Mercury—the closest planet to the Sun—lasts a little under 2 ½ Earth days, and a day on Mars is just an hour longer than on Earth. Farther out, the other planets are much speedier spinners—a day on Jupiter is just 10 hours, the shortest of all. Saturn (11 hours), Uranus (17 hours), and Neptune (16 hours) aren't too far behind.

I'm only six months old on Neptune!

Round trip

The closer a planet is to the Sun, the shorter its journey around it. Mercury, the closest planet to the Sun, completes this loop in just 88 Earth days—giving it the shortest year of all our solar system's planets. A 12-year-old on Earth would be 52 years old if they lived on Mercury! And the longest year? That would be Neptune, where a year is 59,800 Earth days—or just under 164 Earth years.

YOU WEIGH LESS ON MARS THAN ON EARTH

No, the scale isn't just broken! Your weight is how much matter is in your body—your mass—multiplied by the force of gravity. Mars has less gravity than Earth, so you weigh less there.

But I wasn't even trying to lose weight!

What is gravity?

Gravity is the force that pulls you down to the ground on Earth so you don't float off into the sky. It is the same force that keeps the Moon circling around the Earth, and the planets circling around the Sun. It's also the force that holds galaxies together. Hmm, yep, gravity plays a pretty important part in the universe!

Changing weight

Someone who weighs 45kg (100lb) on Earth would weigh only 17kg (38lb) on Mars. Head to the Moon and their weight would drop even farther—right down to 7kg (17lb). That's about the same weight as a small dog on Earth! But head to giant Jupiter and it's a different story ... the same person would weigh around 2 ½ times as much as they do on Earth.

Weight on Earth

Even on Earth, your weight isn't exactly the same everywhere on the planet. Gravity is a bit stronger in some places on the Earth's surface, so without your mass changing you weigh more there. Your weight doesn't change anywhere near as much as it would if you went to a different planet altogether, but it's something that most of us have a much greater chance of experiencing!

We need gravity

Our bodies have evolved on Earth to work in our planet's level of gravity. When astronauts are aboard spacecraft, without the effect of gravity, their bodies struggle to stay healthy. Floating above the ground looks like great fun, but it takes so little effort that it's really bad for us. Astronauts' bones and muscles waste away when they are not used to work against gravity.

FACT 82 NEPTUNE'S MOON TRITON HAS ICE VOLCANOES

The ice volcanoes shoot out what scientists believe is a mixture of liquid nitrogen, methane, and dust. This instantly freezes and then snows back down to the surface.

Er, this moon looks a bit cold.

Brrr ... chilly!

It's so incredibly cold on Triton—the surface temperature is -391 °F (-235 °C)—that nitrogen and methane are both usually frozen solid. On Earth, they are usually gases and have to be made very, very cold before they even turn liquid, let alone solid.

FACT 83 It rains liquid methane almost constantly on Titan, Saturn's largest moon.

94

Pepperoni moon

Io, one of Jupiter's moons, has the most volcanic activity of any object in our solar system. Its surface is covered with hundreds of exploding volcanoes—from far away, it looks a bit like a pepperoni pizza! These volcanoes can shoot jets up to 400 km (250 miles) into the atmosphere, in eruptions so violent that they can be seen by large telescopes on Earth around 630 million km (391 million miles) away.

Not the most appetizing-looking pizza ...

People used to think that the dark patches on the Moon were oceans, like those on Earth.

Mercury and the Moon

Even when a planet or moon no longer has active volcanoes, scientists can tell from clues on its surface whether it once did. Mercury's and the Moon's long-extinct volcanoes have left the remains of their huge lava flows that cooled and turned solid. These show up as dark plains on both their surfaces. The Moon also has large bumps on its surface, called lunar domes, which scientists think were made by lava erupting and cooling slowly in that spot.

Volcanoes on Mars

Millions of years ago, Mars used to have the solar system's largest active volcanoes, and the biggest of all was Olympus Mons. Although it is now long dead, it is still visible on Mars's surface. Olympus Mons is over three times the size of Earth's tallest mountain. In fact, it is so large that if you stood at the top you wouldn't even know you were on a mountain. The mountain slopes would stretch to the horizon and then be hidden by the curve of the planet.

FACT 84

JUPITER AND SATURN MAY HAVE DIAMOND RAIN

Scientists believe that it may rain down diamonds during storms on Jupiter and Saturn. The biggest diamonds would be around 1 cm (0.4 inches) across—big enough for a nice ring!

How to make diamonds

Do you want to become super-rich? Well, first, you should pick up a cow and head to Saturn or Jupiter. Next, wait for a lightning storm. When your cow passes wind, the methane gas will turn into a sooty form of carbon. The soot will fall back down through the planet's deep atmosphere. As it goes, it will be crushed into diamonds, which are just another form of carbon. Ta da!

FACT 85

Beyond our solar system, there is a planet twice the size of Earth which scientists think may be almost entirely made of diamond.

Is space the future of diamond mining?

Diamond seas

Scientists think that once these solid diamonds are formed, they move farther into the planet and eventually become liquid. This would create a liquid sea around the planet's core. Saturn and Jupiter are both gas giants, so their composition is very different to Earth. They look solid from far away but they are mostly made of squashed gases around a small solid or liquid core.

Space mining

Precious gems are big business on Earth—and, in the future, maybe even beyond Earth! The idea is that spacecraft could travel to other planets in our solar system, carrying robot mining ships that are able to collect the diamonds there. The spacecraft would then bring them back to Earth, to make some genuinely out-of-this-world jewels!

Odd weather

In the last 25 years or so, scientists have started exploring all the weird and wonderful planets outside our solar system. These are called exoplanets—and boy, do they have some strange weather of their own! On one planet, it snows rocks and on another it rains burning-hot glass sideways—you wouldn't want to get caught out in that, even with an umbrella. Yikes!

FACT 86 SATURN'S RINGS SOMETIMES DISAPPEAR

Around every 15 years, a trick of the sunlight makes it look to us on Earth as if Saturn's rings have vanished! The last time this happened was in 2009–keep your eyes out for next time ...

Thin rings

Saturn's rings are enormous, big enough to stretch around a planet 764 times bigger than Earth. But they are also very thin—scientists think that in some places they are just 10 m (30 ft) wide. Even at their thickest point the rings are only 1 km (0.6 miles) across, which an average person could walk in around 10 minutes.

FACT 87 One of Saturn's moons has a ridge around the middle, making it look like a giant walnut shell. Scientists think it formed when the moon absorbed some of Saturn's rings.

But I like my rings, I don't want them to disappear!

Disappearing trick

As Saturn moves around the Sun, it sometimes turns its rings edge-on to Earth. The rings are so thin that in a small telescope it looks like they've disappeared altogether! Four hundred years ago, this sight puzzled Galileo, one of the greatest space scientists of all time. Having first spotted the rings in 1610, he was very confused when they seemed to vanish again within two years. For a short time, he even stopped studying Saturn!

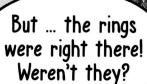

But ... the rings were right there! Weren't they?

Closer look

Saturn's rings are a wonderful sight, but do you know what they're made of? Dust, rock, and ice. Hmm, not quite as glamorous as they seem from a distance ... The pieces that make up the rings vary in size, from a grain of sand to a large-ish house. The rings speed round and round Saturn at great speed. It looks like Saturn has seven rings, but each of these is split up into smaller rings— called ringlets.

Not so special

Saturn is not the only planet in our solar system to have rings surrounding it. In fact, all the other giant planets in our solar system—Jupiter, Uranus, and Neptune—have similar rings. Saturn's are famous for being the biggest and by far the most impressive sight, though. The other planets' rings are much darker and so cannot easily be seen from Earth.

Neptune and its rings

FACT 88

THE MOON IS FALLING TOWARD US!

The Moon has been free-falling toward the Earth for billions of years. But don't panic! It is being pulled sideways at the same time, so it doesn't actually get closer to Earth.

Earth's gravity

What keeps you on Earth's surface instead of floating through the sky and out into space? That's right, it's gravity. The Earth's gravity constantly pulls you toward its middle—and you and the Moon have that in common! It is the reason that the Moon circles around and around Earth, rather than whizzing off into space.

Sideways pull

Aaarrrrghhh, I'm falling!

Gravitational pull toward Earth

We've been over this, you're always falling ...

100

At high speed

If you drop a ball from your hand, it will fall straight down to the ground. But if you throw a ball hard straight ahead of you, and there is nothing in the way, it will travel through the air for a while and then fall downward until it eventually lands on the ground. The Moon is moving at high speed around the Earth, so the downward pull of gravity isn't the only force acting on it.

Falling around Earth

Now imagine if you could throw the ball really fast. It would take a long time to drop down to Earth. If you could throw it superhumanly fast, it would never fall to the ground but just keep moving around and around the Earth. This is what the Moon is doing! It is far enough away, and moves fast enough that it never crashes down to Earth's surface, but instead constantly falls in a curve around Earth.

Balancing act

If the Moon moved a lot faster than it does, it would break away entirely from the pull of Earth's gravity and fly off into space. If it moved much slower, it would be dragged all the way down by Earth's gravity and crash into our planet. The perfect balance between the Moon's speed and its gravity means that it stays in constant orbit around the Earth.

When rockets are launched into space, their speed is set to either join or escape Earth's orbit.

101

FACT 89

SUNSETS ON MARS ARE BLUE

On Earth, we are used to blue sky in the day and red-orange sunsets in the evening. On Mars, it's the other way around! It has a red sky in the day, with blue sunsets.

YOU CAN SEE MARS IN THE NIGHT SKY WITHOUT A TELESCOPE FOR MOST OF THE YEAR.

Blue skies

On Earth, the particles that make up our atmosphere—the layers of gases that surround our planet—partly block the Sun's light and scatter it around the sky. They are much better at scattering blue light than red light, so we see this blue light spread across the sky. This means that most of the time on Earth our sky looks blue.

Look, the Sun's going down. Must be home time!

Reddish sunset

At sunset, Earth's position has moved so that the Sun is now on the horizon rather than appearing high in the sky. The Sun's light now has to pass through so much of Earth's atmosphere that all the blue light is scattered away so that other shades can be seen. This is why sunsets on Earth have their beautiful golden-reddish-orange glow.

Yeah yeah the orange is pretty, but I prefer black and white!

Reddish skies

On Mars, things are a little different. Mars has lots and lots of dust in its atmosphere, which blocks all shades of light about the same amount. This dust is reddish, which makes it absorb the blue light and scatter the red light, so on Mars the sky is usually red.

Blue sunset

The reason that Mars has blue sunsets is to do with these dust particles, too. Looking at the Sun from Mars, there is actually always a blue halo around it, but it is only when the Sun appears on the horizon that its light passes through all the dust and the blue halo is easy to see.

FACT 90
IF YOU PUT SATURN IN A GIANT BATH, IT WOULD FLOAT

You'd need to find a bathtub 60,000 km (38,000 miles) wide to give this a go, but it's true—Saturn is so light for its size that it would float on the surface of water.

I am just so relaxed right now!

SATURN IS A SLIGHTLY SQUISHED CIRCLE SHAPE, WIDEST AROUND ITS MIDDLE.

Huge but light

Saturn is huge, big enough to fit 764 Earths inside it. But although it takes up so much space, the lightness of the materials that make it up means that it doesn't have very much mass for its size at all. Another way to say this is that it has low density. Because it has a lower density than liquid water, Saturn should float on the surface of water, just like a beach ball or a boat does.

Gassy giant

What makes Saturn so light, when it's so huge? In a word, gas. Saturn is a very different sort of planet to Earth—while Earth is made of relatively heavy solids and liquids, Saturn is mostly made of gases, which are much lighter. In fact, Saturn's main gases are especially light ones—hydrogen and helium, the lightest elements in existence (as far as we know).

Helium is lighter than air, so balloons filled with helium float.

The Cassini spacecraft exploring Saturn and its moons.

Mysterious middle

Scientists think Saturn has either a liquid or a solid core in its middle, but they're still not sure exactly which it is. Saturn is a long way from Earth—at its closest to us, it is still 1.2 billion km (746 million miles) away. That's over 3,000 times farther away than the Moon! A spacecraft called Cassini spent over 10 years exploring around Saturn, but there's still a lot for us to learn about the planet.

Tricky test

Can you imagine trying to float a giant swirling ball of gas in a bathtub almost 1,000 times bigger than Earth? It's pretty tricky without a solid surface because we can't even know for sure where Saturn starts and finishes! Well, "floating Saturn" shows us the very real truth that it's less dense than liquid water—but, in reality, it probably wouldn't work quite as well as a nice rubber duck!

BILLIONS OF PLANETS DON'T CIRCLE ANY STAR

"**R**ogue planets" are free-floating planets that have broken away from a star and wander through the universe. They're the rebel runaways of the planet world!

I'm a rebel without a star!

Breaking free

When new solar systems are forming, it's absolute chaos. All sorts of materials swirl around a star in a packed, top-speed confusion, whizzing past and crashing into each other as they go. Most scientists believe that at these times many planets are thrown out of the mix with such force that they leave the system altogether and speed off alone through space.

The red dot in this photo is the rogue planet PSO J318.5–22.

Giant runaways

Rogue planets are big. Waaay bigger than Earth. In fact, the smallest rogue planets are around the size of Jupiter—which is our solar system's largest planet by far, big enough to fit 1,300 Earths inside it. There aren't just the odd few of them wandering around space either—scientists think there may be twice as many rogue planets as there are stars in the universe!

Hello!

Tricky to spot

Despite their huge size, rogue planets are actually very hard for scientists to spot. They do not give off any light, and as they aren't near to a star they can't be seen interfering with the light it gives off—which is how scientists can see many star-circling planets. When rogue planets pass in front of far-off stars, scientists can see the effect of this and work out that they are there, but it is very rare.

Rogue life?

We get our light and heat from the Sun, our nearest star. But rogue planets don't have a friendly nearby star to keep them nice and toasty-warm, so they are very cold. Not quite as cold as you may think, though. Rogue planets produce some heat of their own, maybe even enough to support life—although of a very different kind to anything on Earth ...

JUPITER HAS A STORM BIGGER THAN EARTH

Jupiter's Great Red Spot is a huge, swirling storm that can easily be seen on the planet's surface. It has been going on for 350 years and Earth could fit inside it with room to spare.

Super sized

Jupiter is the biggest planet in our solar system by a very long way—all our solar system's other planets could fit inside it with room to spare! And scientists think this super-sized planet's equally super-sized storm has been raging since more than 100 years before the USA was founded! Earth's longest recorded storm, Hurricane John, back in 1994, lasted just 31 days.

A storm the size of Earth is "little?!"

Neptune's Great Dark Spot

Shrinking storm

Jupiter's Great Red Spot has shrunk to half the size it was when it was first seen. It looks like it's finally dying down after all this time, and scientists think that in 20 years' time we probably won't be able to see it from Earth at all. The thick clouds around Jupiter don't help, as they make it quite hard to see the planet's surface.

Other Great Spots

Neptune and Saturn also have their own "Great Spots," whirling storms that can be seen from Earth. They aren't as reliable as Jupiter's Great Red Spot, though—they seem to disappear and they sometimes appear again in other places on the planet. Saturn has different Great White Spots and Neptune has a Great Dark Spot but only about half the time.

The Little Red Spot

Jupiter has lots of storms whirling around all over its surface. The Little Red Spot is another storm on Jupiter that has been growing since it was first spotted in 2006. It formed when three smaller storms joined together, and it is now around the same size as Earth. So not that little after all!

Imagine if Earth's storms joined together.

A MAN'S ASHES ARE BURIED ON THE MOON

Dr. Eugene Shoemaker was a brilliant scientist who helped to train astronauts going to the Moon. After his death, some of his ashes were carried to the Moon in 1999 and remain there to this day.

Eugene Shoemaker and his wife, Carolyn, spotted comets that had never been recorded before.

Groundbreaking scientist

Shoemaker was a geologist, a scientist who studies rocks. He devoted his life to space, looking at the different objects—such as moons, comets, and planets—in our solar system and how they were formed. He was a world-renowned expert in craters on Earth, other planets, and the Moon, and he trained astronauts to explore the Moon's rocks and craters in a scientific way. He also discovered several comets, which are named after him.

Shoemaker could never join astronauts on the Moon—not during his lifetime, anyway.

Astronaut dreams

Shoemaker had a lifelong dream to travel into space—and, above all, to go to the Moon. He was all set to be the first geologist to ever walk on the Moon, but tests at NASA found that he had a health condition which meant it wasn't considered safe for him to go. Although he had an incredible, scientific career filled with important achievements and awards, he was always haunted by his now-impossible dream.

Craters and comets

Shoemaker had a rich life exploring craters all over the world, often with his wife and fellow scientist Carolyn Shoemaker. It was on such a trip to Australia that he sadly died in a car accident while driving to a remote crater. Shortly before Shoemaker died, he said, "Not going to the Moon ... has been the biggest disappointment in life." But, as we know, his friends and family would put that right in his death.

Finally at peace

Shoemaker's ashes were carried to their final resting place on the Moon in a capsule etched with pictures of Comet Hale-Bopp, the last comet that he ever saw with his wife, and a quotation from Shakespeare's play *Romeo and Juliet.* Although some people have paid to launch their remains into space, Shoemaker is the only person buried anywhere else beyond Earth. His wife said, "We will always know when we look at the Moon, that he is there."

The quote on Shoemaker's ashes capsule reads:

And, when he shall die
Take him and cut him out in little stars
And he will make the face of
heaven so fine
That all the world will be in
love with night
And pay no worship to the garish sun.

FACT 94

GALAXIES CAN EAT EACH OTHER

Big galaxies crash into each other every 9 billion years or so. When this happens, they sometimes swallow up and merge with the other galaxy in order to grow larger. They're space cannibals!

Oi! Get your own gas!

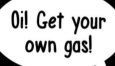

Topping up

Galaxies need lots of gas to make new stars. Smaller galaxies have plenty of gas for this, but bigger galaxies are often running uncomfortably low. By merging with smaller galaxies, these bigger galaxies can be sure that their gas levels are topped up and that they will be able to continue making new stars.

These two galaxies, known as the Mice Galaxies, because of their long "tails," are in the process of merging.

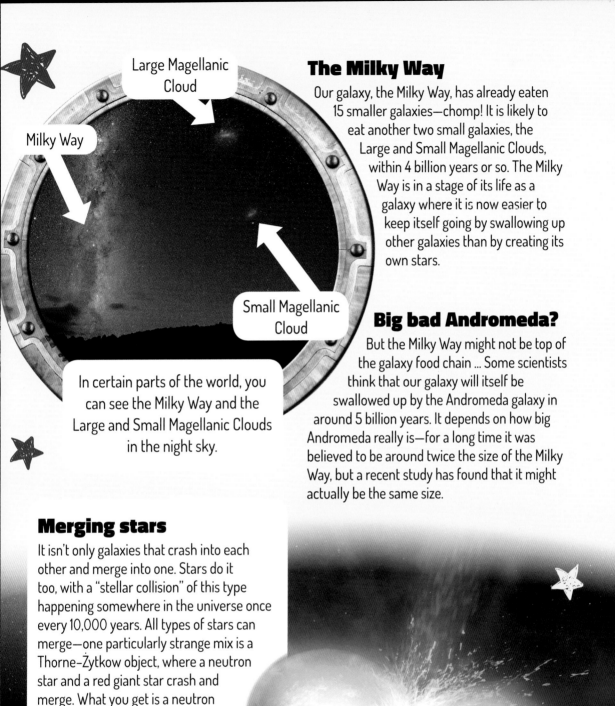

The Milky Way

Our galaxy, the Milky Way, has already eaten 15 smaller galaxies—chomp! It is likely to eat another two small galaxies, the Large and Small Magellanic Clouds, within 4 billion years or so. The Milky Way is in a stage of its life as a galaxy where it is now easier to keep itself going by swallowing up other galaxies than by creating its own stars.

Large Magellanic Cloud

Milky Way

Small Magellanic Cloud

In certain parts of the world, you can see the Milky Way and the Large and Small Magellanic Clouds in the night sky.

Big bad Andromeda?

But the Milky Way might not be top of the galaxy food chain ... Some scientists think that our galaxy will itself be swallowed up by the Andromeda galaxy in around 5 billion years. It depends on how big Andromeda really is—for a long time it was believed to be around twice the size of the Milky Way, but a recent study has found that it might actually be the same size.

Merging stars

It isn't only galaxies that crash into each other and merge into one. Stars do it too, with a "stellar collision" of this type happening somewhere in the universe once every 10,000 years. All types of stars can merge—one particularly strange mix is a Thorne–Żytkow object, where a neutron star and a red giant star crash and merge. What you get is a neutron star in the middle, surrounded by a red giant!

An artist's impression of two neutron stars merging.

THE ROTTEN EGG NEBULA SMELLS TERRIBLE

What's in a name? Well, for the Rotten Egg Nebula there's quite a bit of truth to it. It contains a lot of sulfur, which—when combined with other materials—smells like rotten eggs!

Gross!

What is a nebula?

A nebula is an enormous cloud of dust and gas in space. Some of them are areas where new stars are starting to form, and others are the remains flung out into space by a dying star. Either way, they exist in what we call interstellar space—areas of space in between star systems.

Faraway stink

Don't worry too much about catching a whiff of this space stinker—it's far enough from Earth that we can't smell it at all. The Rotten Egg Nebula is about 5,000 light years from Earth, meaning that it's so far away it takes light 5,000 years to travel that far. To give an idea of how far away that is, it takes light less than 1.5 seconds to travel between Earth and the Moon.

Big change

The Rotten Egg Nebula is interesting to scientists because it's going through a change that they are rarely able to see happening. A red giant star is in the process of dying and violently shedding its outer layers of gas and dust. This change takes around 2,000 years in total, which sounds like a long time but is a blink of an eye in space terms, so it's lucky for scientists to see it in action.

The Hubble telescope took this picture of the Horsehead Nebula.

THE WORD "NEBULA" COMES FROM THE LATIN WORD FOR "CLOUD."

The Witch Head Nebula looks like a witch screaming into space—scary stuff!

Nebula names

The Rotten Egg Nebula does actually have a more polite name—it's also known as the Calabash Nebula. A calabash is a kind of vegetable that has a shape a bit like a bowling pin, which is sort of what this nebula looks like. Other nebula have names that describe what they look like, too—some of the spookiest are the Ghost, Skull, and Witch Head nebulae!

115

THERE MAY BE UP TO 2 TRILLION GALAXIES

Scientists find it hard to agree on how many galaxies there are in the universe. Some think it's 200 million, a computer program said 500 million, and others believe there are far, far more.

The big questions

When scientists try to work out the answers to huge questions about space, such as "How many galaxies are there in the known universe?", they have to use the information that people have already gathered and use it to make predictions. Computer programs now help scientists to do this in more complex and accurate ways than were possible in the past.

It's out of this world, man!

Seen and unseen

Scientists got to the figure of 2 trillion galaxies by creating models in a computer program, based on the Hubble telescope's 20-year collection of images. The Hubble telescope shows us more of space than ever, but scientists believe that only 10% of the known universe's galaxies are visible to us now. The figure of 2 trillion galaxies takes this into account, so it's a lot higher than the number of galaxies that have actually been seen.

Computers are a huge part of space science, from controlling missions to running simulations with data.

Galaxy shapes

The galaxies that we can see at the moment don't all look the same. Most are in the shape of a spiral or an egg, but some have no particular shape at all—they just look like a vague assortment of stars, gas, and dust spread out in all directions. Our galaxy, the Milky Way, is a spiral galaxy.

Sombreros and tadpoles

Scientists have had great fun naming some of the galaxies that we've discovered so far. There is the Sombrero Galaxy, the Tadpole Galaxy, and the Sunflower Galaxy, for a start. The Milky Way's name comes from an Ancient Greek myth about the goddess Hera spraying milk across the sky. In China, it is called the Silver River and in the Kalahari Desert in Southern Africa it is known as the Backbone of Night.

The Sombrero Galaxy is named after the wide Mexican hat that it looks like!

A BLACK HOLE COULD STRETCH YOU LIKE SPAGHETTI

Don't get too close to the edge of a black hole! If it's a smallish one, its gravity will pull hardest on the closest part of you and streeeeetch it away from the rest.

Spaghettification

This all sounds terrifying, but at least it gives us a great word—spaghettification! This describes how an object falling into a black hole is stretched, and sometimes ripped apart, by the force of gravity. An object spaghettified by a black hole would be trapped inside it, stretching out farther and farther for ever and ever.

It's one way to grow taller!

White holes, the opposite of black holes, should be possible, but we haven't found any yet. They would only give out light and matter, nothing would be able to enter them.

No escape

A black hole has very strong gravity, which gets much stronger the closer you get to it. Once you have been sucked into the black hole, you can't escape it—no matter or light can. That's why black holes are invisible.

Spaghettifying stars

It's not just humans who are at risk of this spaghettification—we know that it happens to stars. In fact, we've seen black holes tearing stars apart in this way! Stars are only at risk if they stray too close to the edge of a black hole, though. This is called the black hole's "event horizon," and it's like the edge of a waterfall—the closest anything can get without being pulled down into it.

Exploring a black hole

There may be no escape from a black hole, but if you'd like to at least be able to have a look around inside rather than be totally spaghettified, make sure to pick a big one. The gravity of very large black holes is enough to suck you in whole. Most galaxies have the largest type of black hole—our galaxy, the Milky Way, has one called Sagittarius A in its middle.

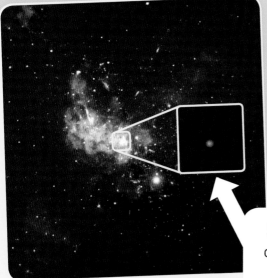

Scientists think this blue dot was a flash of light, caused when an asteroid fell into Sagittarius A and was torn apart.

THERE COULD BE AN INFINITE NUMBER OF UNIVERSES

Some of the most cutting-edge ideas about space can sound like something out of science fiction. To make sense of the strangeness of space, scientists have to open their minds to all sorts of possibilities.

Rules don't apply

Scientists are learning more about space every day, but sometimes instead of this answering any big questions it just opens up lots more new questions! We know that lots of things about space don't fit in exactly with our rules for how things work on Earth, so scientists have to think creatively about the different models that could make our universe work the way it seems to.

Not alone?

One of the most out-there ideas about our universe is simply that it's not the only one. Most scientists until now have worked on the assumption that nothing else exists beyond or alongside our universe—that our universe is literally everything. But until around 100 years ago, we thought that our galaxy was the only one in existence, whereas now we know it's just one of billions upon billions ...

Multiverse theory

The idea that there is more than one universe is known as the "multiverse" theory. Within this idea, there are lots of possibilities for how these multiple universes might be arranged. Some scientists have thought about them as bubbles within bubbles, some as a patchwork quilt stretching on forever, some as slices of bread side by side within a larger loaf.

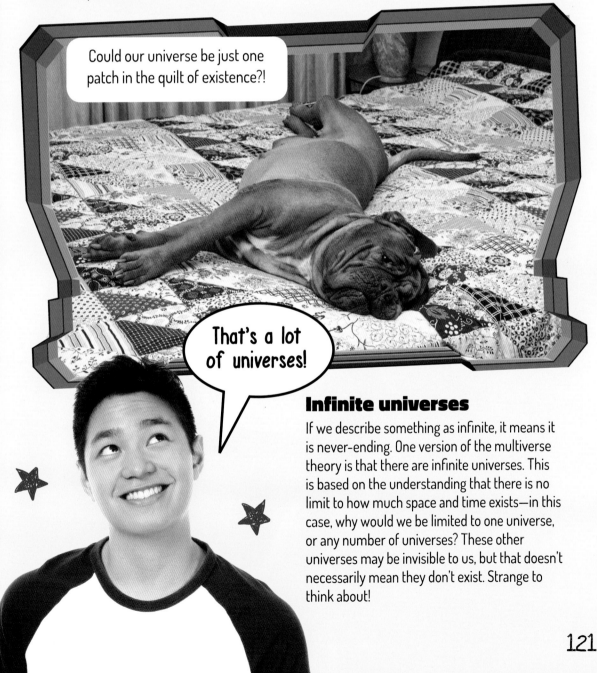

Could our universe be just one patch in the quilt of existence?!

That's a lot of universes!

Infinite universes

If we describe something as infinite, it means it is never-ending. One version of the multiverse theory is that there are infinite universes. This is based on the understanding that there is no limit to how much space and time exists—in this case, why would we be limited to one universe, or any number of universes? These other universes may be invisible to us, but that doesn't necessarily mean they don't exist. Strange to think about!

FACT 100

WE MIGHT HAVE FOUND ALIENS WITHOUT REALIZING

One of the biggest questions about the universe is "Are we alone?" The answer? We still don't know. Scientists don't think they've found alien life, but they admit they might not recognize it if they saw it.

Seeing in space

It can be tricky for scientists to see exactly what's going on far off in space. When things are very distant from Earth, it's not like looking at something through binoculars on Earth. They can't always get a clear, detailed picture of what they're trying to see, so it might be tricky to see signs of life. Sometimes scientists can't actually "see" an object at all, but they know it's there from how it affects its surroundings.

Hey ... HEY ... I'm over here!

NASA IS CURRENTLY RUNNING MISSIONS TO TRY TO FIND ALIEN LIFE IN SPACE.

Unfamiliar beings

It can be hard to imagine something completely outside your own experiences. When scientists look for proof of life elsewhere in the universe, they are searching for evidence based on their knowledge of the needs and qualities of living things on Earth. But alien life might be so different to any sort of life we're familiar with that scientists are missing the very different signs of its existence.

Simple life

When we imagine alien life, we often think of creatures fairly similar to ourselves—they may look different, they might be bright green with huge pulsating brains, but they are intelligent life forms. Actually, many planets and moons may be able to support some kind of simple life, like the bacteria we have on Earth, but the chances of finding intelligent life is far lower.

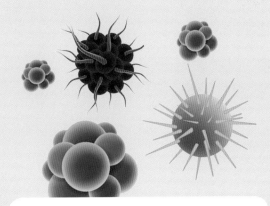

Alien life may be simple, tiny creatures like bacteria—or something else entirely!

Extreme Earth

Scientists have found living creatures surviving in conditions on Earth so extreme that we thought it was impossible for any life to exist there. They have discovered simple life forms called microbes living in burning-hot pure acid in Ethiopia's Danakil Depression, one of the hottest places on Earth. Studying these extreme-living microbes helps us understand how and where alien life might be found in space, in conditions where humans couldn't survive.

The Danakil Depression might look like somewhere on another planet, but it's right here on Earth!

FACT 101

95% OF THE UNIVERSE IS MISSING

Less than 5% of the universe is made of matter and energy as we understand it and can see it. The rest of it is invisible dark matter and dark energy. Gulp.

Missing matter

Scientists have realized that in space lots of things aren't quite adding up ... For instance, galaxies are spinning so quickly that the gravity from their visible matter shouldn't be strong enough to hold them together. They should have torn themselves apart a long time ago, but they haven't. Scientists think this is because they have more matter, which is invisible to us—they call this dark matter.

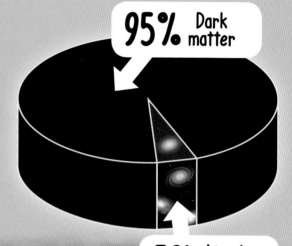

95% Dark matter

5% Atomic matter

Spinning so quickly means we have to hold on tight!

Dark energy

Dark energy is even more mysterious than dark matter—and scientists think it makes up over 70% of the universe. While scientists have some ideas about what dark matter might be—strange and not-yet-seen particles—they struggle a lot more to explain dark energy. The reason they think it exists is because the universe is growing and pulling galaxies farther apart, so there must be a greater force acting against the gravity that holds galaxies together.

Astronomical voids

There are huge areas in space where there are no or very few galaxies—scientists call them astronomical voids. But what looks like empty space to us might be something that we just don't understand yet. There is a giant Cold Spot in the universe, a cooler area that scientists think has many of these voids, and one idea is that it could be the spot where our universe crashed into another one!

Still learning

Essentially, dark matter and dark energy are what scientists think bridge the gap between what we have measured in space and how we see the universe behaving. We are still only just starting to understand many things about space, and how its strange forces and structures work. Many ideas that scientists have today might turn out to be wrong or to be only one part of the answer—that's how science develops.

Glossary

asteroid A small rocky object made up of material left over from the birth of the solar system.

astronomical void A vast area of space containing very few galaxies or none at all.

atmosphere A shell of gases kept around a planet, star, or other object by its gravity.

Big Bang The way in which many scientists believe the universe began—a huge, hot explosion that expanded out all the matter in the universe from one tiny point. Since this explosion, the universe has continued growing outward and is still doing so today.

black hole A superdense point in space, usually formed by a collapsed core of a giant star. A black hole's gravity is so powerful that even light cannot escape from it.

comet A chunk of rock and ice from the edge of the solar system.

dark energy An unknown form of energy that many scientists think exists throughout the universe, acting in opposition to gravity and causing the universe to expand faster and faster over time.

dark matter A strange, invisible substance that forms most of the mass in the universe.

dwarf planet A world, orbiting a star, that looks like a planet but does not meet certain criteria needed to make it a true planet.

exoplanet A planet orbiting a star outside our solar system.

galaxy A large system of stars, gas, and dust with anything from millions to trillions of stars.

gravity A natural force created around objects with mass, which draws other objects toward them.

International Space Station An artificial satellite that circles around Earth with astronauts from all over the world living on board and carrying out scientific experiments.

Kuiper Belt A ring of small icy worlds directly beyond the orbit of Neptune. Pluto is the largest known Kuiper Belt Object.

light year The distance light travels in a year—about 9.5 trillion km (5.9 trillion miles).

magnetar A small, very dense, strongly magnetic type of neutron star.

meteor The glowing path of a small piece of rock or other matter that has entered Earth's atmosphere. It appears as a fast-moving streak of light in the night sky, and is also known as a "shooting star."

meteorite A solid piece of an object from space—such as an asteroid, meteoroid, or comet—that has fallen to the Earth's surface.

meteoroid A small rocky or metallic object moving through space.

microgravity Very weak gravity, as you would find inside a spacecraft circling around Earth.

Milky Way Our home galaxy, a spiral with a bar across its core. Our solar system is about 28,000 light years from the monster black hole at its heart.

Moon Earth's closest companion in space, a ball of rock that orbits Earth every 27.3 days. Most other planets in the solar system have moons of their own.

nebula A cloud of gas or dust floating in space. Nebulae are the raw material used to make stars.

neutron star The core of a supermassive star, left behind by a supernova explosion and collapsed to the size of a city. Many neutron stars are also pulsars.

observatory A building or room that contains a telescope or other scientific equipment used to study space.

Oort Cloud A spherical (ball-shaped) shell of sleeping comets, surrounding all of the solar system out to a distance of about two light years.

orbit A fixed path taken by one object in space around another because of the effect of gravity.

planet A world, orbiting a star, which has enough mass and gravity to pull itself into a ball-like shape, and clear space around it of other large objects.

protostar A pressurized cloud of gas that is on its way to becoming a true star, but can still fail and become a brown dwarf if it can't pull in enough gas as it forms.

pulsar A fast-spinning neutron star whose intense magnetic field forces its radiation into two narrow beams that sweep around the sky like a lighthouse. From Earth, a pulsar appears as a quickly flashing star.

quasar A distant, active object in space that has a very bright core and gives out a huge amount of energy.

red dwarf A small, faint star with a cool red surface and less than half the mass of the Sun.

red giant A huge, brilliant (very bright) star near the end of its life, with a cool, red surface. Red giants are stars that have used up the fuel supply in their core and are going through big changes in order to keep shining for a little longer.

rocket A vehicle that drives itself forward through a controlled chemical explosion and can therefore travel in the vacuum of space. Rockets are the only practical way to launch spacecraft and satellites.

rocky planet An Earth-sized or smaller planet, made up mostly of rocks and minerals, sometimes with a thin outer layer of gas and water.

satellite Any object orbiting a planet. Moons are natural satellites made of rock and ice. Artificial (man-made) satellites are machines in orbit around Earth.

solar system The eight planets (including Earth) and their moons, and other objects such as asteroids, which orbit around the Sun.

spacecraft A vehicle that travels into space.

spiral galaxy A galaxy with a hub of old yellow stars (sometimes crossed by a bar) surrounded by a flattened disk of younger stars, gas, and dust. Bright newborn stars make a spiral pattern across the disk.

starquake A violent shaking and ripping of the crust of a type of star called a magnetar, similar in some ways to an earthquake on Earth.

supernova An enormous explosion marking the death of a star much more massive than the Sun.

telescope A device that collects light or other radiations from space and uses them to create a bright, clear image. Telescopes can use either a lens or a mirror to collect light.

white dwarf The dense, burned-out core of a star like the Sun, collapsed to the size of the Earth but still intensely hot.

Index